"Micháel has written one of the best and most practical books on church growth. I have applied his principles and seen our church grow both in quality and quantity. It's must reading for any pastor."

—**Dr. Che Ahn**, Senior Pastor, Harvest Rock Church

"Michael Fletcher has written a current book on issues that face every single church if it is going to grow. The book is clear, concise, and a guide for anyone wanting to take their church to the next level. Michael is a practioner of what he writes. Read it, do it!"

—**Bob Roberts Jr.**, Senior Pastor, Northwood Church, and Author of *Transformation* and *Glocalization*

"Every pastor with a heart and hunger for a growing church of multiplying believers should grab this book and read every page—now! Then, get ready to grow big time."

—**Dr. Dick Eastman**, International President, Every Home for Christ

OVERCOMING
Barriers to
Church Growth

MICHAEL FLETCHER

🖋 BETHANYHOUSE
Minneapolis, Minnesota

Published by Bethany House Publishers
11400 Hampshire Avenue South
Bloomington, Minnesota 55438

Bethany House Publishers is a division of
Baker Publishing Group, Grand Rapids, Michigan.

Printed in the United States of America

ISBN 978-0-7642-0687-0

The Library of Congress has cataloged the hardcover edition as follows:

Fletcher, Michael.
    [Leadership transitions for growth]
    Overcoming barriers to growth : proven strategies for taking your church to
the next level / Michael Fletcher.
        p.   cm.
    Originally published: Leadership transitions for growth. Colorado Springs,
CO : Wagner Publications, 2003.
    Summary: "An experienced pastor describes common barriers that growing
churches face and what transitions and leadership strategies are necessary for
continued growth"—Provided by publisher.
    ISBN-13: 978-0-7642-0294-0 (hardcover : alk. paper)
    ISBN-10: 0-7642-0294-4 (hardcover : alk. paper)
    1. Christian leadership. 2. Church growth. I. Title.

    BV652.1.F48   2006
    254'.5—dc22   2006026446

To my wife, Laura,
who has patiently walked with me through
the many years of lessons learned the hard way.
Your love, loyalty, faith, and wisdom have been my strength.

To those countless pastors and elders
who daily labor together to win
for Him the reward of His suffering.
May this book serve to make your journey more fruitful!

MICHAEL FLETCHER is the senior pastor of Manna Church in Fayetteville, North Carolina, and leads Grace Churches International, a network of 319 churches in 43 countries. Since Michael became pastor of Manna in 1985, it has grown from 350 to 5,000 active members. He has a passion to see other pastors step beyond their current leadership barriers and watch their churches become all God intends for them. He and his wife, Laura, have eight children and six grandchildren and make their home in Fayetteville, North Carolina.

Contents

Contents

Foreword by
C. Peter Wagner

MOST PASTORS IN AMERICA, and in other countries where Christian churches exist, will spend a career of thirty, forty, or more years leading small churches. Around 90 percent of them will never see a regular Sunday attendance of more than two hundred. The average weekly church attendance in America is well under one hundred.

Surfacing facts like these are in no way intended to put down small-church pastors. These pastors are essential for the body of Christ to be all that God intends it to be. And heavenly awards for pastors will not be distributed according to church size. Many small-church pastors will end up having more stars in their crown than some of the megachurch pastors who have become household names.

God will reward pastors, as He will reward all believers, on the basis of how, in this life, they exercised faithful stewardship of the gifts that He gave them. Because small churches are essential for the health of the collective body of Christ, God has gifted many pastors to lead small churches. Most small-church pastors are right where they are supposed to be.

But not all. Some pastors of small churches have been given the necessary gifts to lead larger churches, but for various reasons they have not been able to move into their true destiny. Here is where this book comes into the picture. Michael Fletcher, whose church sees a weekly attendance in the thousands, has personally broken the barriers that ordinarily stall out church attendance. Most others like him, who have also broken the barriers, lead so intuitively that if you asked them they would not be able to tell you how they made it happen. They would say, "It was the grace of God," or words to that effect; words that offer little or no practical guidance for those who would follow in their footsteps.

Michael Fletcher is different. Not only does he have what it takes to pastor a large church, but he also has the ability to analyze how he got there and to spell it out clearly for others. If you are a pastor or church leader, and if you are not satisfied with the status quo, this book will be a tremendous help and encouragement to you.

Let me make a few more comments about this book.

First, I would point out that the church growth movement is now almost forty years old. Researchers throughout this period have discovered that there are actual numerical barriers to the growth of a local congregation, and various people have postulated about a dozen of these supposed barriers. Only two have withstood the test of time: the one-hundred- to two-hundred-member barrier and the seven-hundred- to eight-hundred-member barrier. This book is completely up to date. It is the first church growth book to focus on these two proven barriers to church growth.

My second comment may sound like hyperbole, but it is not. Of the hundreds of books that have been published on church growth,

I would say that this is the best guidebook for pastors today. For one thing, it brings together the wisdom of years and applies it to twenty-first century churches. It is better than any of my church growth books, because my books are now considered old. For another, Michael Fletcher has a commendable ability to carve away the fat and get right down to the meat. A superb quality of this book is its compact size, with power-packed information on each page. As you read it, I promise that you will not feel like you are wasting your time.

Have you reached your full destiny as a church leader? *Overcoming Barriers to Growth* will help you answer that question and will show you how to advance to a new level.

C. Peter Wagner
Senior Professor of Church Growth
Fuller Theological Seminary

God Has a Plan for You and Your Church!

WHEN A NEW CHURCH begins, it is often planted by those who, in the early days, do everything as friends. The church is their mutual project and they "own" it together. The core people arrive early on Sundays to set up the chairs. Because the sound system lives in the worship leader's trunk, that person is always the first to arrive and unlock the doors in the rented facility. (Except that one time he was on vacation and took the whole system to the beach.) When folks arrive, everyone knows everyone else by name—even the children are known by everyone! It's easy to spot newcomers, who are usually swarmed upon and talked about over lunch. Sometimes they may actually become lunch. It is also easy to tell if someone is missing. There simply are no cracks through which anyone can fall. When a mom is sick or gives birth, no meals have to be organized—friends just show up with a dish. Relationships grow and strengthen as the early challenges are overcome.

Need more space? No problem; the men of the church give up their Saturday afternoon and bust out a wall or two to make more room for the kids or to add more chairs for worshipers. After church it's potluck ("blessing" in some churches—they don't do "luck"), then folks grab paintbrushes to coat the newly constructed but not-quite-so-straight walls. Some people paint and some point out missed spots, but while the paint goes on the walls and some on the floor, painters and pointers alike dream aloud of the days when the church will really grow.

"This is church life as it was meant to be!" Everything is perfect. You can always get to the pastor, you know everyone by name, and you make the sacrifices necessary to make the church better. Yes, everything is perfect—until the one thing happens that can ruin it all. New people come, and now they tend to stay.

No one can remember when it started to happen. One day you came in and it seemed that the place was full—new faces without names. And children? "Not sure, but I wonder if the parents are serving in the nursery." Everyone is supposed to take their turn, but not everyone does, so before long, a leader is appointed to make sure everyone is on some sort of list, and the new people are duly instructed. There are too many chairs for the committed few to set out, so a special team is formed. A list appears in the bulletin (never needed bulletins in the early days) of people who are scheduled to clean the building, because the four ladies who used to do it every week needed a break.

In one area after another, leaders are appointed and teams are formed to facilitate the flow of ministry. The church is growing, but no one knows why. Worse yet, no one knows what will stop the growth. Who has time to ask questions like that? There are meetings to be held and new leaders to be raised up.

Soon elders are appointed to help the pastor "carry the load." At first, that is their only assignment—to help out. But what does that mean? Does an elder's role ever change? It seems like Scripture indicates that having elders in place will help the church grow. And it isn't long before that starts to prove true. With elders on board, helping to carry the load—that is, doing the ministry—the pastor has more time to be creative, and the people get more of the attention they crave. The church happily grows on. What used to be owned by everyone is now owned by the elders, and the people concede that to them. After all, the elders are the ones who were there from the beginning and made the greatest sacrifices. Great people with great families, they, along with the pastor, have the authority in the church. They can do anything—even stop its growth.

Stop its growth?! Why would they want to do that? The truth is, they don't want to stop its growth, but they will. They are totally unaware that a barrier to growth awaits them—a barrier caused by their own success. Not only do they create the barrier, they are, at the same time, the key to getting over it! If the pastor and elders will adjust the way they relate together in leadership and realign some of the internal structures they built into the church, they can keep right on growing. Most churches don't make those adjustments for two reasons: (1) They don't see the barrier, so they don't see the need; and (2) they don't want to change what they perceive made them successful in the first place.

This is where the trouble starts. The church slows in its growth, even though it continues to slowly add people. Unfortunately, folks are leaving at about the same pace. Under the surface, frustration mounts, especially among the leaders. The pastor attends a seminar held by a successful church on how to become a megachurch—a dream of his since before he planted this church with a few close friends. His new "vision" is met with resistance, especially from the one elder who works in corporate America. "While we know you to be a man of God, brother, the job of creating vision belongs to the whole eldership, not just the senior pastor." Another elder comes back from vacation with an idea gleaned from visiting his daughter and son-in-law's church. His excitement over what he perceives to be the key to moving forward in growth is interpreted by the pastor as dissatisfaction and a growing lack of commitment. Still another elder reminisces over dinner about the glory days of old and ponders aloud if churches really need to grow after all.

Feeling a need to keep things in line, the pastor reaches for greater control and, in an effort to exert his God-given authority, announces a new initiative from the pulpit without consulting the elders. The next elders' meeting is really the next embers' meeting as members smolder, acknowledging the rightness of the new idea but burning over the wrongness in how things were handled. Eventually, embers turn to flame when, in an entirely different discussion, the pastor suggests that the church consider buying a new computer system. Not immediately recognizing their reaction as stemming from strife over the issue of control and authority, the elders decide to tighten the purse strings and reject the computer idea.

In my travels inside and outside our network of churches, I have seen this same scenario occur time and again. Sadly, this type of interaction and jockeying for control is far too common in local churches. What began as life-giving, rewarding, and even fun has become dead, boring, and stressful.

Most churches stuck in nongrowth patterns lose people not only from the periphery but, unfortunately, also from the core. Often, over time, the very ones who made the church what it is depart, distraught over what they feel it has become or, in some cases, hasn't become. They leave to join churches that are not only growing larger but are also more vibrant expressions of the body of Christ. These growing churches seem to move along effortlessly. Everything they do seems to work, while making anything work in the nongrowth church is a major effort. These painful endings to long-standing relationships only add to the strife and frustration in churches that are needlessly stuck behind a growth barrier. In some instances, hopelessness and a sense of defeat set in, replacing the youthful, expectant faith of the past with a desire simply to hold on and wait for better days.

Everywhere I go I see the same problems. Pastors are frustrated with their leadership teams, and the leadership teams are frustrated with their pastor. Typically the church is not growing, and the mechanisms required for problem-solving have become ensnared in a quagmire of confusion.

Every church, as it pursues the vision of the house, goes through phases in its journey toward growth. Along the way, the local church will encounter certain numerical barriers to growth. C. Peter Wagner has well documented these barriers and widely published the tried and true principles for breaking these barriers. Having helped local churches through these barriers for years, I have noticed that in all churches the transition period prior to reaching the growth barrier requires *internal* change in the unseen mechanisms of the function of the church, namely, in the relationship between the senior pastor and the local church leadership team or eldership. If those changes are made, then the church is prepared to address the growth barrier successfully. If the internal changes are not made—and most leaders never detect the need for internal restructuring—the church will never make it through the barrier no matter what *external* changes they make.

Whenever I talk to pastors, it never fails: we always get around to talking about their frustration with trying to bring a vision to life. Whenever I talk to eldership or leadership teams, it never fails: they are struggling, at some point, with the pastor. They all love each other and are committed to the success of the church, but over time something has gone wrong. That "something" is a failure to recognize a transition. And now the tension caused by needed, yet neglected, restructuring has affected precious long-term relationships.

On the road to becoming a megachurch there are three key stages of leadership structures or configurations and two major transition points. Tension mounts as these transition points are approached. These times of tension, interestingly enough, occur at the same point as the major growth barriers. If pastors and leaders properly anticipate these transitions and adjust appropriately, stress can be reduced and leadership teams can work together to experience growth instead of working against each other.

Growth Stages

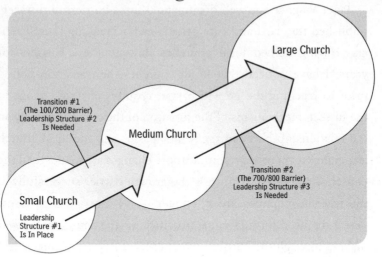

In this book you will find tools—proven and effective—that will help you pilot the church through these barriers and on to new vistas of church life that are life-giving, rewarding, and fun once again.

For the record, I am not interested simply in helping churches get larger. I am interested in helping them become healthy, from the inside out, so they *can* grow. If the internal structures of the church are not properly aligned, the rest of the church will not function properly either.

This book comes out of my experience, which has been framed in the evangelical/charismatic segment of the Christian family. Some of my language is shaped by that experience. However, I believe that the kinds of situations I describe that impede growth are not limited to the type of churches I know well. Over the years, pastors from a wide variety of ecclesiastical backgrounds have testified to this fact. These truths work in any local church because they deal with people and how people work.

My passion is to see people released into ministry—not just leaders, but every church member. I want to see people becoming who God created them to be and functioning

> **We don't have time to sit in board meetings and fight over who is in charge. We have a world to change!**

maturely in all their gifts and callings. I want to see the church released into the world, acting as a vehicle for the aggressive advance of the kingdom of God on earth. I want to see the church change the world, and average, everyday believers being the ones used by God to do it! For this to happen, the local church has to be structured in a way that will best facilitate the development and release of God's people. We don't have time to sit in board meetings and fight over who is in charge. We have a world to change!

The Power
of Vision

NOT LONG AGO I asked a group of some thirty young men whom I was training for full-time ministry a question that brought varied and thoughtful answers. "What is the most important thing to make a church or ministry successful?" Although each was convinced his answer was correct, and most identified a piece of the puzzle for a church's overall long-term health, all but three missed the mark. If we have learned one thing from the church growth movement over the years, it is that effective leadership must be present for growth to occur.

What is the magic of leadership? Why is it so important in taking a church or ministry where God wants it to go? The answer is this: It isn't really leadership itself or even the personality of the leader that moves a church or ministry along, but the natural outworking or application of that leadership gift within the person of the leader. Simply put, it is what good leaders naturally do that produces and sustains momentum. Let me explain.

Effective leadership always expresses itself in two ways: vision and faith. This is true in the secular and sacred worlds alike. Left alone and placed in charge of anything, a leader will begin to dream about the future and fashion an ideal in his mind that is brighter than the present. At first, the dream is only a dream, distant and unattainable. But over time, as he turns this dream around and around in his head and heart, a confidence begins to grow that what he pictures can become a reality. Soon he begins to share this new vision with others, who, at first glance recognize the improbability of the new ideal but still are strangely drawn toward a belief that it can actually come to pass. Somehow, they can see what the leader sees.

Employees or church members begin to work with a calm assurance that the new plan will work and a new future will be formed. People who before came to work to earn a paycheck, or came to church to enjoy a service, are now marshaled into a force to accomplish a task, and the business or congregation moves forward as a result. The leader made this happen, but not by simply being in charge. Progress occurred because of the natural manifestation of true leadership among a people: the expression of vision and faith.

THE FORMATION OF VISION

The formation of vision is a solo project. It begins with a dream. Dreaming is easy for most, but turning dreams into an attainable vision is the product of leadership. What is vision anyway? In a Christian context, vision is the ability to see what God wants to do in a given situation. In reference to the local church, vision is the ability to see what God wants to do in and through a group of people. The leader *sees* the future.

Vision has everything to do with sight, but not natural sight. Vision is seeing through the eyes of the heart. True vision is far more powerful than natural sight. A leader filled with vision can look beyond small numbers, financial difficulty, and impossibilities of the present and see, with clarity and passion, the future as if it has already come to pass. For the leader, present problems are temporary inconveniences to be tolerated on the road to what will certainly be a more glorious future. The future is just around the corner. In seeing it, the leader can almost touch it.

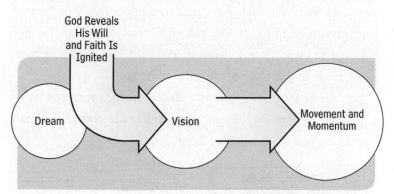

What, then, is the difference between a vision and a dream? Everything! Most people dream. But a dream without faith is a fantasy. There is nothing wrong with having a dream, with meditating on a fantasy about what God *could* do. In fact, all vision is drawn from the well of dreams. The difference is that vision is a statement of what God *will* do. When leaders first conceive possibilities for the future, they are like everyone else—dreaming of a better tomorrow. But somewhere along the line, something more happens. God begins to impart faith to the leader. The dream mutates and becomes more concrete.

Through prayer, the leader gives God access to the dream he holds in his heart. God then "speaks" to the leader by breathing faith into those parts of the dream that reflect God's plan for the local church he leads. This faith makes the vision seem real, attainable. To those looking on, the vision seems unreachable at first, but when the leader speaks and shares his heart on the matter, faith acts like a contagion—others begin to believe that the impossible is now possible.

Without the element of faith, a dream remains the creation of the human mind—a fantasy. Many people, enamored with a dream, chase it, hoping it will come true. But the Bible says, "He who works his land will have abundant food, but the one who chases fantasies will have his fill of poverty" (Proverbs 28:19). Fantasies never materialize because they inherently lack the faith necessary to mobilize one to work effectively, whereas the faith required to create a real vision inspires the visionary and those around him to put their best effort forward.

Let me be clear. The senior leader is not the creator of vision but rather its caretaker. Dreams are largely the creation of man, but vision, true vision, comes from God.

> **Fantasies never materialize because they inherently lack the faith necessary to mobilize one to work effectively, whereas the faith required to create a real vision inspires the visionary and those around him to put their best effort forward.**

Many times, after a seminar on growing the local church, I have seen senior pastors set their hearts to find God's vision for the house. Some show up the next day with a vision in hand, all typed out. They missed the most important point and short-cut the process. As a result they merely tip *their* hand to God and lose out on the impartation of faith, leaving their vision powerless. The hard work of vision is in the wrestling with God!

A leader prays for God's vision, waits, receives nothing, prays some more, dies to self, waits, wonders, prays. Slowly faith begins to rise, slowly the pieces come together. The picture is rarely what he first thought it would be and is always larger than he would have constructed himself. It is no longer man-sized.

Further, he finds that he is not at the center. This vision is God-sized, and it will take His power to produce it. The pastor knows it is God's idea and He will bring it to pass, no question about it! The leader is passionate in his belief, and because of that, others catch the vision and work to see it occur. In the end, only God will get the glory.

This may be the hardest but most important job of the senior pastor—finding God's vision for the local church he leads. The Bible says, "It is the glory of God to conceal a matter; to search out a matter is the glory of kings" (Proverbs 25:2). God isn't being unkind in "hiding" the vision within himself—just the opposite. In concealing it, He forces us to seek Him, and in seeking Him, we find more than a simple plan. We are infused with faith. Remember, it is faith that attracts others to the vision; it is faith that enables them to believe that it can actually occur; it is faith that will motivate them to work toward that end. The best thing God could do for us is to hide the vision in His own heart, because in seeking it out we become the leader that others follow!

All of this dreaming, praying, believing, and seeing happens in the heart of one person. That is why the formation of vision is a solo project. One person dreams and interacts with God over that dream. God sorts through the ideas contained in the dream, breathing life into some of them, reconstructing the dream into a vision of His formation, all the while imparting faith. Some believe this type of faith is actually a gift to leaders for just this purpose—making them the guardians of a vision from God to the end that God's people are mobilized into action as a unit.

Moses serves as a beautiful example of the singular nature of vision formation. When God decided it was time to deliver His people from bondage, He called on one man—Moses. It wasn't that Moses was inherently special—he was simply selected. God gave him specific instructions and commissioned him to lead. Moses anticipated conflict with some Israelites who might have challenged his authority, but God was undaunted. Moses was to be the man. And though Aaron was allowed to stand at Moses' side, it was Moses alone who met God at the burning bush and Moses alone who ascended the mountain for direction.

When Aaron and Miriam challenged Moses as the solo voice of visionary leadership, God responded with sharp criticism of their attitudes. When Korah and his allies said they should have a hand in shaping the course for the Hebrews to follow, the ground actually opened up and swallowed two hundred fifty of them! When God wanted to give direction to the people, He called Moses alone to the top of the mountain and into the Tent of Meeting.

It has always been God's pattern to use one leader who would speak for Him in guiding the people into the vision of His destiny for them. Before Moses, there were Abraham and Noah. After Moses came Joshua, Samuel, Gideon, and Deborah. They were followed by others: David, Daniel, and Jeremiah, to name a few. Some were quick to step to the fore, while others recoiled from the prospect of solitary leadership, but all were selected by God to cast a vision for the people. Never was the formation of vision the product of a committee, and every attempt at such was met with God's displeasure.

THE THREEFOLD LAW OF VISION

Not only is the formation of vision a solo project, but the operation of vision is also in the hands of one leader. Every vision that comes to pass goes through three stages: articulation, unification, and mobilization. This is what I call the "Threefold Law of Vision." Nowhere in the Bible is this seen so clearly as in the early ministry of Nehemiah. Having heard of the state of disrepair of the walls surrounding the Holy City in his homeland far away, Nehemiah, the cupbearer, requested leave of the king to return and rebuild. With his petition granted and a host of exiles in tow, Nehemiah returned to Jerusalem to reconstruct necessary ramparts of defense and restore the city's dignity. Consider the following from the narrative:

> By night I went out through the Valley Gate toward the Jackal Well and the Dung Gate, examining the walls of Jerusalem, which had been broken down, and its gates, which had been destroyed by fire. Then I moved on toward the Fountain Gate and the King's Pool, but there was not enough room for my mount to get through; so I went up the valley by night, examining the wall. Finally, I turned back and reentered through the Valley Gate. The officials did not know where I had gone or what I was doing, because as yet I had said nothing to the Jews or the priests or nobles or officials or any others who would be doing the work.
>
> *Then* I said to them, "You see the trouble we are in: Jerusalem lies in ruins, and its gates have been burned with fire. Come, let us rebuild the wall of Jerusalem, and we will no longer be in disgrace." I also told them about the gracious hand of my God upon me and what the king had said to me. They replied, "Let us start rebuilding." So they began this good work. (Nehemiah 2:13–18, emphasis added)

Notice first that Nehemiah went alone, at night, to examine the walls. It was not a move of independence but a desire to avoid clouding his mind with opinions of the "committee." It also provided his heart time alone with God to formulate a plan of God's design. No doubt those initial moments of seeing the walls were devastating. He probably asked himself what he had gotten himself into. He didn't need opinions, he needed God!

Soon Nehemiah rehearsed the graciousness of God and encouraged himself. Then he began to "see" what was possible. Faith ignited in his heart, and he knew that what he saw in his heart could be done, even though what he saw with his eyes so dramatically contradicted that proposition.

Second, notice the pronouns in this passage: "I went out . . ." "I moved on . . ." "I went up . . ." "I turned back . . ." "I." "I." "I." The solo aspect of acquiring a vision is clearly indicated here. But it is only solo from a human perspective. Nehemiah was not alone—the gracious hand of God was upon him. God was gripping his heart at every turn. No doubt this is why he went out at night. What can a man see at night? He had no flashlight; there were no streetlights. He was in the dark, literally. His purpose was not so much to see the walls as it was to "see" what God would say to his heart. He needed to be alone with God. He needed God's light to shine on him.

Sad to say, knowing my nature, had I been in Nehemiah's shoes, the first thing I would have done is call a meeting of all the key leaders in which a processional review of the walls was followed by an equitable distribution of tasks. Nehemiah had the authority to require these men to comply and do the work. Instead, he was reaching for something higher, something that would motivate the people of God to work toward the goal with joy and sacrifice, with passion and perseverance. He was reaching to unlock the power of vision. How many pastors have made the mistake of thinking, *I'm the senior pastor, sent by God to these people. They should just listen to me and follow!* This line of thinking is often coupled with a corollary question, *Why won't they just follow?*

Third, notice how the pronouns shift from first person to third person. In the end, the people own the vision and the people do the work. What "magic" did Nehemiah possess to procure such favor? None. He simply applied the Threefold Law of Vision!

Step One: The Law of Articulation

Nehemiah cast the vision to the people. He pointed to the need and suggested a bold solution. He made it so clear, they could see the possibility. I call this first step the "Law of Articulation." The guardian of a vision has to be able to accurately articulate the vision so that "the many" can *see* it as one man. I often say, "You can't go where you can't see." Leaders must take time to make sure the people get it or they won't be able to, or want to, follow it. Don't rush the process. It involves more than making people aware of a vision.

This step is where visionaries are often weak. Since the vision is so clear to them, they falsely assume that others see it with the same clarity. Leaders need to use more than just the Sunday morning pulpit to communicate a vision. Write the vision in a short, clear statement and put it everywhere—bulletins, guest packets, letters (in an amended form), etc. We have our church's overall vision statement printed in a very artistic format, framed, and hung all over the building (even in the bathrooms!). Distill the vision into a sentence and place it on letterhead, as part of your signage, in the text of most of your printed material. In every way possible, articulate the vision.

Step Two: The Law of Unification

Step Two is a must. I call it the "Law of Unification." The timing of God is determined by the pace at which the people of God rally around the vision. Most pastors jump from Step One to attempting to bring about the vision virtually by themselves. They are frustrated by the reluctance of people to "get on board."

Unfortunately, the very nature of vision works against a pastor at this point. The leader's faith makes the thing seem so doable, so close, that he impatiently reaches for its accomplishment and alienates the very ones necessary for its successful implementation.

Many factors come into play when seeking unification: the leader's skill in articulating the vision in terms of doable goals or steps; the health of the body to whom the vision is proposed; and a host of other points of consideration. Notice in the account of Nehemiah: "*They* replied, '*Let us* start rebuilding.'" The goal at this stage is to rally the troops. If this doesn't happen, the leader need not waste time in critical thought toward the people. Rather, the leader needs to return to the "mountain" for additional sessions with God.

Years ago we were in the articulation stage of incorporating small groups into the life of our congregation. The overall goal was to transition into being a cell-based church. The bulk of my teaching during this period centered on New Testament concepts captured in the Greek word *oikos* (meaning "house" or "household"). In modern times, this equates to a person's sphere of influence, the web of relationships of which God has made us a steward. I wanted people to take responsibility to "reach" those naturally within their reach.

That year the Valentine's banquet included a skit that turned out to be a parody of me. A couple of the guys put on pig masks and did a takeoff on the word *oikos*. They instead used "oink-kos." Of course, everyone saw the ruse and heartily laughed, but none harder than me. When my wife asked why I was laughing so enthusiastically, I simply leaned over and replied—with no small sense of satisfaction—"They got it." Step Two was complete!

Step Three: The Law of Mobilization

Finally, once a group buys into a vision and makes it their own, Step Three, the "Law of Mobilization," comes into play. The people, seeing and believing a vision they had not considered before, step into action. The work of the whole—the force of many—brings into reality a vision that was seen with the eyes of one heart but now is seen with the eyes of all.

There is no hard-and-fast rule as to how long this threefold process will take. In our case of transitioning to a cell church, I taught about the concept for a whole year before even starting one cell group. In the end, it was a five-year shift. And yet when we launched a massive campus ministry, the vision was cast, people jumped on board, and the funds started to flow in just one week!

The local church is an organization, but even more, it is a living organism. Therefore, leaders must embrace the idea that the Threefold Law of Vision is an organic process. Vision mechanically imposed on a local church will, in time, either be rejected or ignored. Do not ignore or rush through this non-negotiable law.

THREE KEY QUESTIONS

While the formation and operation of vision begins in and flows through the life of one, it is clear that others must enter the picture for the second and third laws to operate as required. This is where the leadership team comes in. While Nehemiah acted alone in hearing from God, he immediately shared the vision with those who were leaders in Israel. Moses was chided by his father-in-law for being a one-man show and not including the leaders God had provided to serve the people (see Exodus 18).

Applying these principles to the local church, I see three questions that must be settled in order to avoid the stress and strain that unnecessarily plagues most leadership teams. If these issues are ignored, we will find ourselves looking a lot like the nation of Israel. We have elders meetings where the Aarons and Miriams, or worse, the rebellious sons of Korah, reach out to take what God has not given them. We attend meetings where senior pastor Moses unwisely tries to hold on to what rightly belongs to the leaders God has gathered around him.

What?

The first question for leadership is "What?" What is God's plan for this house? What is the vision, the mission for which this church has been established by God? The answer, as I have already shared, is given by one person—the senior leader. While many others in a local church may hear from the Lord and add to the ideas surrounding the implementation of the vision, the vision itself flows through the one God called to lead them. When Jesus speaks to the seven churches in the second and third chapters of Revelation, while it is clear that the messages are to the entire church in a particular city, the Lord addresses His comments to the "angel of the church." Most Bible scholars believe that to be the pastor of the church. In speaking to the church, He speaks through the leader.

When?

Left alone, having the "what" communicated by one leader is a very dangerous proposition. Sadly, we have seen many abuses of authority in the body of Christ over the years. Fortunately, the what question is balanced by two others, the first of which is "When?" After leaders come down from the "mountain," their greatest friend and worst enemy is the vision residing in their heart. Their faith to see the thing come to pass both empowers and deceives them. Faith creates that charisma that draws people to do what they never could before. But faith is very "now" oriented and can produce a drive and an impatience that is unhealthy for local churches.

This is why God has added other leaders—elders in the biblical context (or deacons in some ecclesiastical settings)—to help implement the vision. They are to ensure that the steps required to accomplish a grand task are laid out at a pace the "ewes and lambs" can keep. These are trusted counselors. Understanding their place, they would never restrain the leader from walking in the God-given calling to lead. But they do, in providing the counsel of multiple elders, help the leader break the plan into workable parts on a reasonable timetable.

Wise leaders, while somewhat disappointed that a vision cannot come to pass as fast as they would like, or even as fast as they perceive possible, acknowledge the valuable role of elders finding the best sense of pace. They know that implementing something too quickly can lead to unnecessary failures and turn the people against that which God has given. And without the people, as we have already seen, nothing lasting will happen in bringing the plan to reality.

How?

The third and final question that must be settled is "How?" The Bible clearly instructs us that "in the multitude of counsellors there is safety" (Proverbs 11:14 KJV). A vision is a lofty goal, a picture of the future. Those who are natural visionaries can easily see such a picture and happily work toward it. But the majority of folks are not natural visionaries and need to be shown the next step—the one right in front of them. While they may lose contact with the overall vision, they easily attend to the task at hand, working to accomplish one goal at a time.

Elders help the leader break the vision into parts that people can manage and design a plan that produces a string of successes—thus creating unstoppable momentum. The leaders are taken from among the people and feel what the people feel. They are invaluable at this point. Being included in the practical "how" of the vision draws elders/leaders into ownership and releases them to lead among the people. Wise senior pastors who embrace the counsel of elders actually multiply themselves among the people. The voice of vision, once spoken by the leader alone, is now spoken on the lips of many in settings and circles beyond one person's scope of influence.

NOT JUST THEORY

In the introduction, I talked about three stages of leadership structures as well as transitions and tension points. The idea is that internal leadership structures will need to change in order for the church to break through the barriers that threaten to hold them back. While these internal structures—namely the way in which senior pastors and leadership teams or elders interrelate—need to undergo adjustment, some things will never change. The "what" of vision will always belong to the senior pastor and the "when" and "how" will belong to the senior pastor and the elders as partners in leading the church to growth and health.

These ideas are not just theories to me. I have learned by experience, both mine and others'. In my early years, I had plenty of heartache trying to bring my vision to life. I worked and worked but didn't get anywhere. Now our momentum is seemingly unstoppable. My relationship with the elders and their relationships with each other have changed in keeping with what I have learned over the years. As a result, at the time of this writing, I am pleased to share that there has not been one angry word shared in an elders' meeting in twenty years! Not one angry word, not one move for control. While we are not *nearly* perfect and many times stumble through the process, even in frustration we do it together, all pursuing the same vision and all confident we are in the place we belong. In the next chapter, I'll share how this can be your experience as well.

Every Stage Requires Change

CHAPTER TWO

I WISH I HAD KNOWN these things when I first started as a senior pastor! I knew that creating and casting vision was my responsibility, but I had no clue about how or even why to include others in the process. I was eager to hear from God about His plan for us, so I spent lots of time on the mountain seeking God's face and dreaming about His future for us. No one told me that faith would result from taking the dream continually before the throne. No one told me that a real vision would eventually emerge as faith and a clear picture of God's will comingled in my heart. It just happened. What they did tell me was that I needed to include the other leaders in the house in creating a plan to bring about the vision. I didn't listen. I had the vision God had given me. I reasoned that God and I were a majority, and the elders just needed to get on the wagon and ride. If I needed their help, I would ask them. I was *so* humble.

At twenty-six years of age, I had stepped into the senior pastor role of a three-hundred-fifty-member church where I had previously served as an elder, youth pastor, and associate pastor for three years. I should have known better. These elders and pastors were guys I loved and trusted; we were teammates, most with far more experience than I. They were behind me all the way, and because of that, they believed the vision.

Even so, they could see straight through the web of deception that had spun around me. They tried to speak words of wisdom to me. "Brother, this is all good, but you are trying to go too fast with this. The sheep are not able to keep up with this pace." "These are great goals, and I hope every one of them comes to pass, but what plan do you have to make it happen?" I didn't listen. I felt I couldn't listen. I didn't know I was supposed to listen. They should be listening to me! I responded by trying harder to sell the vision.

The real trouble was that I didn't know how to relate to the elders. I had been an elder, but now that the table was turned, I couldn't seem to interact with them in a way that brought the best out of them and provided me with the help I felt I needed.

I was committed to having elders in the church because the office and function is clearly spelled out in Scripture (i.e., Acts 14:23; 1 Timothy 3:1–7; 1 Peter 5:1–4). Further, I knew the "one-man show" was risky and unbiblical. So I tried to feel my way along.

At first I included the elders in everything, but that bogged me down and drove me crazy. Then I backed up and included them only in key decisions, while I provided the direction and drive on daily affairs. This made them feel left out and prompted them to reach for more. In response, I felt they were unfairly questioning me. (I am so glad those days are over!) Finally, in frustration, I confided to a member of the pastoral staff who had formerly served as a senior pastor himself. "I don't know what to do with the elders! I see them in Scripture, but what we are experiencing cannot be what God had in mind." With the voice of a sage, my trusted friend said to me,

"Michael, you are not the leader you one day will be. Right now you must decide how you see the elders functioning in the local church. Are they advisors? Are they laypastors? Are they overseers? If so, what and how do they oversee? They will take their cue from you."

I learned my first lesson. In our church it was up to me to set the tone and direct the elders as to how they were to relate to the congregation and to me as the senior pastor. I was clueless as to how exactly to proceed, but I knew for certain that the ball was in my court.

DIFFERENT STRUCTURES, INSIDE AND OUT

Over time, I began to see certain stages in the life and development of a local church. A small church is very different from a medium-sized church. In the same way, a medium-sized church is very different from a large church. The real difference is not the size but in how the internal functions of the church operate. In fact, size is the least of the differences! Everything about these various-sized churches is different.

Some people think the church that started with just a few families two years ago should and will be the same church ten years from now with the exception of having more people attending. Not so! Let me illustrate. When a church is new, if there is a change in the schedule, a few phone calls will set things right. But that won't work when there are one hundred fifty people in the church. How we communicate has to change.

As a church grows, overall needs remain the same—fellowship, Bible study, prayer, outreach, assimilation, and communication—but how leaders attend to these needs must be adjusted.

In a church plant, if the pastor decides the church needs more fellowship, a call today results in a church picnic tomorrow. With one hundred fifty members, it takes a little more planning. With two thousand members, picnics are not possible at all, but fellowship is still important. Mechanisms that provide for fellowship have to be carefully built into the philosophical fabric of a ministry, an enterprise not undertaken overnight.

If church leaders do not change the way in which they address the functions of church life, the leaders will actually hinder growth. For example, people may enjoy getting that phone call about the picnic from the pastor; and when the church is small, this is a nice pastoral touch. But as the church grows, the pastor has a harder time keeping up with everyone. It's difficult now to tell those who are "in" from those who are "almost in." In calling people the pastor knows, he might leave out one or two families that are on the verge of joining. Now a message is sent that is exactly the opposite of what is intended. While some are being powerfully touched and included, others are being excluded.

In all likelihood, similar messages are going out to new people through other channels of ministry. When the new folks stop coming, church members, and even leaders, often shake their heads and say, "It's a shame those folks don't have what it takes to fit in here."

Things have to change for a church to continue growing. I have heard it said that growth brings its own problems. But those problems all have to do with areas in the local church that must be adjusted in order for it to continue to go forward.

Today, folks have the notion that copying the megachurch model on the outside will produce mega growth. I have visited a number of churches that have all the outward signs of a megachurch—power point sermons, television screens in the hallways, state-of-the-art Web sites, etc.—but they still number in the one hundred fifty range. In fact, studies show that 75 percent of Protestant churches in North America have less than one hundred fifty members.

The real issue isn't merely getting external ministries in line but readjusting internal operations of leadership. A human being will not be able to grow simply by adding more skin and muscle. Simultaneous with the growth of soft tissue is the growth of the skeletal structure. Simply put, old ways of operating will keep us in the old way. If we want to break into the new, new structures must be developed.

CROSSING OVER INTO A NEW STAGE

To cross over into a new stage, leaders must understand what lies ahead and make the necessary realignments *before* they expect to move to a new level of growth. Look into the mechanisms of leadership in the next stage and build accordingly, in advance of hitting the next barrier to growth. We will explore this idea more deeply later. What is important here is that we grasp the notion that we must build for the next stage before we reach it.

In analyzing the stages of church development, we'll examine three key ideas: (1) how the elders relate to ministry, (2) who actually does the ministry, and (3) how decisions are made. The chart on page 48 summarizes the following pages.

> To cross over into a new stage, leaders must understand what lies ahead and make the necessary realignments *before* they expect to move to a new level of growth.

What isn't addressed here is the internal ministry structure of a church plant. That is because a church plant is like an amoeba of church life. All the functions of church life take place inside one small cell. Everyone in the church is connected to everyone else. Leadership in the church plant is often in the hands of one who receives input informally from a few trusted mature friends. Usually, there is no formal structure. In terms of how ministry happens, a church plant is an "all hands on deck" operation. Anyone and everyone does whatever it takes to move the group forward. As soon as leaders are identified (whether they are elders or not) and responsibilities are doled out, the church plant begins to take on the characteristics of a small church.

SMALL CHURCHES

1. How Do the Elders Relate to Ministry?

In a small church, the elders are the ones who are actually "doing" the ministry. These are the people who have been raised up to help carry the load. These laypastors literally take responsibilities from the pastor. As the church grows from the church-plant stage and further develops inside the context of a small-sized church, this transfer of responsibility is vital. Ministry is multiplied and people are helped. At the same time, the pastor is released to function in more particular areas of gifting.

It is likely that the eldership team is comprised of the key players of the various functions of ministry in the local church. The worship leader, Sunday school director, finance person, small-group leader, and perhaps even the youth leader, among a number of other possible position heads, are probably elders. In this way, the elders are very hands-on in ministry. Simply put, they are the ones who do it. If someone needs counsel, it will be an elder who counsels them. Elders are the ones who visit the sick, lead evangelism teams, teach the classes, and so on.

2. Who Does the Ministry?

In a small church, the most mature and capable people are often those who are designated as elders. In most cases, these are the ones who are most qualified to minister in public ways. Often, at least in the early days, few others are able to serve. Even as others are raised up, the elders have also grown in wisdom and competence in ministry, so the people naturally continue to look to them. Consequently, the elders are the ones who actually do the bulk of ministry needed in a small local church.

3. How Are Decisions Made?

The elders make all the decisions in a small church: the big ones—when and where to buy property, who gets hired, etc.—as well as smaller decisions. The elders might be the ones who review the curriculum for Sunday school. They will also decide on colors to paint the hall in the nursery area. I was in an elders' meeting where changing the color of the front door was discussed for over an hour! All the decisions pertaining to the local church, in some way, make it through the agenda of an elders' meeting in a small church. If they don't, and someone begins to call the shots inside the ministry they oversee without including an elder at some point, they are likely to be seen as independent at best and rebellious at worst.

MEDIUM CHURCHES

1. How Do the Elders Relate to Ministry?

After a church breaks through the 100/200 barrier of "active" members (more on this term in the next chapter), ministries and competent leaders usually multiply, so some, if not many, of the oversight responsibilities may now be delegated. It is unreasonable for all these new leaders to be considered elders, so a second tier of leadership begins to informally develop. The pastor and elders sense that accountability is not what it was, and they now feel somewhat out of touch. In the "old days," each major ministry was led by a person who also served as an elder. Now most of what is done in the church is led by someone else.

Often elders are then appointed to oversee sections of ministry led by others. One elder might be in charge of all small groups, while another might have oversight of the Sunday school and children's ministries. Someone else oversees music and sound, while another watches after the men's, women's, and singles' fellowships. These elders may not actually attend these functions each week, but they work with the leaders who do. From a leadership perspective, rather than their hands being "on" ministry, their hands are "in" ministry. Rather than doers, they have become overseers.

In order for a church to reach this level of development and growth, more than one pastor is serving on staff. In this stage, it is likely that there will be several full- or part-time staff pastors. In most churches, all of these pastors are considered elders. In fact, in most situations, it is considered automatic that a staff pastor is also an elder.

2. Who Does the Ministry?

The people in the church, under the oversight of an elder, are the ones who actually do ministry in a medium-sized church. No doubt the elders themselves are also involved in the function of touching people, but this is now according to gifting and personal interest and not exclusive to the position of elder. Before, they did everything because they had to. Now that others have been raised up to lead, elders are free to minister as individuals in the local church and as regular members because they are drawn to a particular ministry.

3. How Are Decisions Made?

In a small church, the eldership team makes *all* decisions together, but in a medium church, it makes *ministry* decisions. Sunday school curriculum formerly chosen by the whole group is probably now selected by the elder overseeing children's ministry in consultation with those who serve as leaders in this arena every week. The elders then approve or disapprove of the choice. The elder who oversees the youth ministry might discuss the destination of the group's annual mission trip with the youth leadership and then present it to the elders as a whole for approval—again, not hands-on but hands-in. The deacons, or a committee, might deal with room colors, for example, but they don't make a final decision until they make a formal or informal presentation to the board of elders.

LARGE CHURCHES

1. How Do the Elders Relate to Ministry?

A large church has multiple staff members. Competent pastors and ministers serve the church in various areas of concentration. The larger the church gets, the more specific these concentrations tend to become. For a church to get to this level, some of its pastors will not serve on the eldership team. At this stage, the role of eldership is almost strictly governmental. In fact, as a church moves from small to medium, and medium to large, the ministry role of eldership decreases, and the

TRANSITIONS AND TENSIONS IN GROWTH

Changing Roles and Functions of Elders

100/200   700/800

Size of the Church	Small Church (under 200)	Medium Church (200–700)	Large Church (over 800)
Elders' Relation to the Ministry	• "DO" the ministry • Hands-on • Act as lay-leaders	• "OVER" the ministry • Hands-in • Act as over-seers	• "ADVISE" the ministry • Act as advisors
Who Does the Ministry	• The elders. (There may be no one else to help—must do it themselves.)	• The elders are over the ministry. • Church members do the ministry. (Elders organize and lead groups of people to perform the ministry.)	• The staff is over the ministry. • Church members do the ministry. (Elders are more removed and more like a board of directors—may not even be aware of all that is going on ministry-wise. Elders deal only with the big matters.)
Decision-making	• Elders make all the decisions.	• Elders make ministry decisions.	• Elders make policy decisions.

governmental role proportionately increases. Consequently, the role of elders in a large church is primarily advisory in nature. While the skill of ministry is the quality that sets elders apart in a small church, and the ability to lead is paramount in a medium-sized church, it is the wisdom of the elders in the large church that is at a premium.

2. Who Does the Ministry?

Pastors and staff in a large church oversee the ministries in much the same way elders do in a medium-sized church. Things happen way too fast to keep the elders up to date on all the details of daily church life, so the staff works together to operate the many ministries. As a church grows larger, there is no way to hire enough staff to actually do all of the ministry. Members, overseen by layleaders who are under the care of a particular staff pastor, are the primary ministers.

Churches slice the pie in different ways. Some divide their church into geographic districts and place all the functions of the church—benevolence, cell groups, counseling, etc.—under a pastor who oversees that particular district. Other churches adopt a departmental model and place pastors as specialists over certain operations of the church. Such departmental divisions might fall along the lines of cell groups, education, worship and fine arts, missions, etc. Still others use a combination, but all end up seeing their pastoral staff primarily as equippers, overseeing and releasing people into ministry—leading leaders.

3. How Are Decisions Made?

It is extremely unwise to attempt to turn a large ship too fast. In fact, leaders who are prone to this style of leadership are probably not going to be able to lead a church to more than seven or eight hundred members. That is not to say that large churches are inflexible. Large churches can function just as fluidly as any medium-sized church—even more fluidly in some cases. Rather than waiting for decisions to be made at weekly elders' meetings, the staff can make decisions on a daily basis. In fact, to maintain momentum, they have to.

The elders in a large church concern themselves with policy decisions. To make daily decisions, the staff needs clear direction concerning what they can and cannot do, and the kinds of decisions they can and cannot make. Policies give direction and provide "tracks" upon which the staff may run. Policies are designed to facilitate the vision in the local church and give practical direction to the members who oversee and serve in the various functions of church life. "He who pays the piper calls the tune." So those who frame the budget decide the direction of the church. Final approval of financial matters comes from those whose mission is not strictly defined in terms of a district or some specialized area of ministry, but by those whose eyes are on the health of the church as a whole, and whose passion is the pursuit of the vision of the house. In the end, the elders are those who "call the tune."

WHAT DOES NOT CHANGE

In all three stages of growth, one thing never changes—the roles of the senior pastor and the elders in relation to the vision. The senior pastor is always responsible for the "what," and the pastor and the elders work together to formulate the "when" and "how."

What I have shared above is in no way to be considered exhaustive in reference to the role of elders in the local church. We simply looked at how they function in relationship to three issues at various levels in the development of the local church. Our purpose in so doing was to provide insight into the stages of growth so leaders can prepare properly for the transitions required to move from one stage to another. Between each stage is a seemingly impenetrable barrier, the nature of which is the subject of the next chapter.

Church Growth Dynamics and Breaking Barriers

FOR A LONG TIME, the chart on page 48 had no numbers on it at all. I simply defined small, medium, and large churches in terms of the dynamics I saw operating within them. Actually, the chart was first put to paper (on a napkin to be exact) in an effort to describe to a pastor of a church that was bumping up against the 100/200 barrier why he and certain members of his leadership team were having conflicts. (I carried that same napkin all over the country, working with churches, until one of my pastor friends put it into a form akin to what you see in this book.) Everywhere I went, pastors and leaders asked me to define small, medium, and large by assigning a numerical designation to each. I strongly resisted because I felt the key was not in gauging how well a church was doing relative to a static number but how it was progressing in modifying its internal structures to allow for continued growth and development.

I had long studied church growth and considered C. Peter

Wagner and others to be gifts to the body of Christ in providing helpful tools and invaluable insight into the dynamics of growth in the local church. My reluctance to put numbers on the chart had nothing to do with rejecting the ideas I had learned. Indeed, when we were approaching the two-thousand-member mark, our church hosted Dr. Wagner and his seminar on breaking the 100/200 barrier for the purpose of strengthening the churches in our city and our own network of churches. My reluctance had more to do with the doubts I had concerning the universal application of what I had discovered. I wanted to look into the workings of more churches before I assigned numbers to the transition points. Over time I became convinced that the transition points I was seeing in church after church directly corresponded to the barriers outlined by church growth experts.

So what are these barriers and how do they work? First, let me hasten to say that I am no expert here. All that I share on this point I have learned from those who truly are the experts. Also, I am not a theoretician; I am a practitioner, so I have applied these ideas in our own local church and shared them with a host of others, with excellent results. These barriers are real, and the way over them is tried and true. Many have gone before you. It is impractical for me, at this point, to tell you to put down this book and attend a seminar or read certain pages in a number of books. I will attempt to articulate what I have learned about these barriers from study and practical experience.

While there are numerous barriers to growth, most local churches need only concern themselves with two: the 100/200 barrier and the 700/800 barrier. In both cases the numbers have to do with how many active members a church has. Some define this in terms of people who actually attend the church. Others concentrate on the number of adult members. I like to use the term *active* members. Many churches add people's names to the rolls and then remove them only upon death or a request to transfer membership to another church. Other churches purge their rolls annually by a variety of methods. Those names that remain after the purge are considered members of the church.

An active member in my view is one who can be counted upon to participate in some way in the life of the church. These people regularly give, participate in a small group, and/or attend weekly services at least once or twice a month. They see themselves as attached to the local church (perhaps not as tightly as the pastor would like) in a living, organic way, not just as a name on the roll.

Once a church has one to two hundred active members, or seven to eight hundred active members, it has reached a barrier to growth.

THE 100/200 BARRIER

What makes a small church successful is what will eventually halt its growth. Everyone in the small church knows everyone else. This creates a tight community, composed largely of the kind of people "we like"—people who are "like us." This makes fellowship close and builds a family-type atmosphere.

Small churches, without realizing it, intuitively resist growth at some point since continued growth threatens the closeness they so enjoy. After a certain number of relationships, a person just doesn't have room for more. Folks cannot remember everyone's name but somehow feel they should. Not knowing everyone, and the underlying guilt that says we should, produces an awkwardness that actually pushes others away. Those who are "in" are in, and those who are "out" are not likely to break in without a tremendous amount of tenacity. Small churches fear that growing might destroy the family they have become.

There are all sorts of unwritten rules in a small church—ways things are done and not done. In the old days, we called ourselves "Mannanites" since the name of our church is Manna Church. People who came were not considered one of us until they had mastered all the hidden rules. No one actually said this, and there wasn't a secret book of rules in some locked drawer. But knowledge of these do's and don'ts is what separates newcomers from the "real" members, no matter whose name is on the membership roll. While no one wants to admit it, the unwritten-rules game is really a control game—the way people in small churches protect what they have worked so hard to build.

Everyone in a small church connects to the pastor, as shown in the following diagram. There are other respected leaders in the church, but members look to the pastor as the go-to person. He has the final say on all matters pertaining to church life. This is what some call the Shepherd Model.

The Shepherd Model

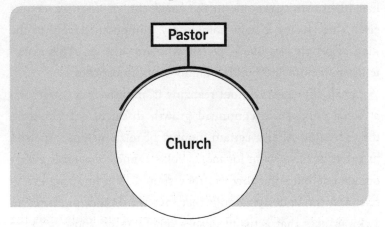

But one person can only effectively oversee so many others. Some have speculated this to be the main reason churches face a barrier at one hundred to two hundred active members. From a sociological perspective, a single pastor has reached the limit at this number. As the church reaches two hundred active members, the phone rings off the hook. The poor pastor becomes exhausted just thinking about the prospect of growing larger.

For a church to break through the 100/200 barrier, at least three things need to happen:

1. **The people must accept the fact that they will not be able to know everyone in the church.** This does not mean that they must give up a sense of family, but it does mean they will have to learn to experience it in other ways. Properly done, this barrier can be broken without destroying the great fellowship members have been enjoying. New circles of fellowship must be developed, and even multiplied, to prompt continued growth.

2. **The people will have to become inclusive of others, and unwritten rules will have to be supplanted with clear methods of communication.** In order for this to occur, new space will have to be created in people's hearts for new people. Surprisingly enough, this is more a structural concern than a relational one. You can't make people want more relationships when they already feel full. New internal structures will create opportunities for more people to plug in.

3. **The pastor will have to switch from a Shepherd Model to a Rancher Model.** Notice in the following Rancher Model diagram there is more than one circle. This does not mean that there is more than one church meeting in the same location. Nor does it mean that the church has actually split into two. It does mean that another leader has been raised up to whom people can connect as another "go-to" person. In this leader's sphere of responsibility, that person is the final answer. This leader has the authority to act and lead as a delegated authority of the senior pastor.

I have talked with pastors who say, "I have this really great youth pastor (or music minister or associate) on staff, so we must already be in the Rancher stage!" That is not necessarily so. The

The Rancher Model Diagram #1

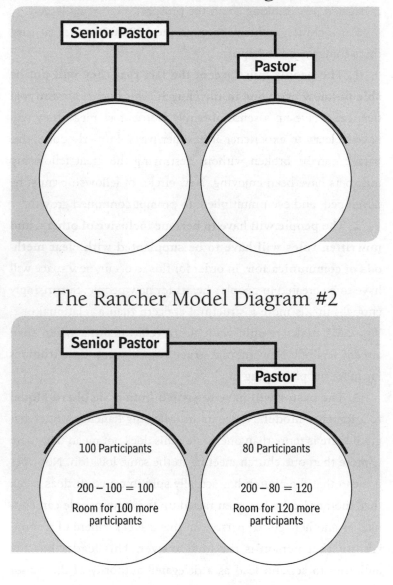

The Rancher Model Diagram #2

real question is, do folks look to that staff member as their pastor? Do they recognize that person as another leader in the house, or as the senior pastor's junior partner in ministry? Are they confident seeking that person's counsel on personal matters? In short, is there a good portion of the church "connected" to someone other than the senior pastor? This idea scares many pastors, but this must happen in order for a church to grow.

Depending on the types of structures established in the church, a congregation that plateaued at 180 active members because its circle was full now may have 100 in one circle and 80 in another, with plenty of room to grow in both!

To continue growing, all the church has to do is add more circles, which obviously means adding more leaders. Usually these leaders will be paid members of the pastoral staff, although in a smaller church a strong elder can sometimes function in this role, but this is rare. And even then, as the church grows, paid staff will have to be hired.

The Rancher Model Diagram #3

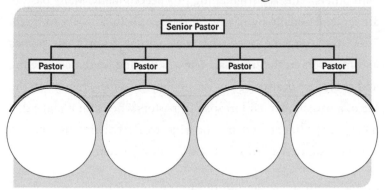

It is my opinion that moving from the Shepherd Model to the Rancher Model is the most important aspect of breaking the 100/200 barrier. In fact, I believe that this infrastructural adjustment is all that is needed to facilitate the people "shifts" shown in the Rancher Models. When new circles of fellowship are created that are sized to allow for others to join, and more proactive communication processes are implemented, people (who are like sheep) will naturally follow. I am not taking a low view of the people of God; my contention is that it is easier to create new structures than to try to make people ignore sociological laws that tend to govern human behavior. When the church was moving toward the 100/200 barrier, people were added and accepted into the fellowship of the church. In the early days, there was a feeling that there was always room for more. The goal of shifting to the Rancher Model is to allow for that dynamic to occur once again.

The First Shift: The Pastor

Leadership structures, then, are the ones that must undergo the most drastic change in order to break the 100/200 barrier. The first shift that must occur is in the mind of the pastor. The pastor must embrace the idea of sharing leadership and ministry with others. This is a frightening prospect to many. Many pastors are fed emotionally by having all the people look solely to them. They like being the ones who visit newcomers in their homes and members in the hospital. They like doing all the counseling and could not bear to be out of the loop in some situation in the life of a parishioner. Unfortunately, pastors who cannot make this mental adjustment will not be able to lead their churches to make the jump over this first and greatest barrier.

The Second Shift: The Eldership

The second shift that must occur is in the minds and hearts of the eldership. New leaders are going to have to be brought into ministry. That means the elders can no longer be the ones who do all the meaningful tasks. A second tier of leadership must be developed, so responsibility and authority must be delegated. This is crucial. I find that most bottlenecks to growth happen right here in the interaction between the pastor and the elders or among the elders themselves. We'll discuss this in detail in chapter 5, but I have found very few eldership/leadership teams where all the members were functioning as they should according to their stage of growth. Trouble is always the result, and the church suffers as a consequence.

Elders in a small church often struggle at two main points: (1) They do not want to give up what they perceive to be the control of the church to people they esteem to be less competent than they, and (2) they fear the pastor's growing authority. As the church grows, the role of the senior pastor becomes less of a ministry position and more of a leadership position. The more responsibilities the pastor delegates, the greater his authority, and members both feel and respond to that. Elders who have to make all the decisions, who keep their hands on all of the ministry (thus controlling it), who seek to limit the pastor's authority, will not be able to lead a church through this barrier.

The Third Shift: The Congregation

The final shift that must occur is in the mind of the congregation. People want to be led and fed. As long as those two things are happening, they will follow a leader wherever the leader takes them. Personally, I think the people of God as a whole want to grow, want to love God more, want to learn His ways and become like Him.

Everything that happens in the leadership is magnified among the people. When leaders sneeze, the sheep catch colds. When things aren't going well, leaders—myself included—tend to blame the people, when the lack is often really found in our failure to clearly lead or feed them along the way. It isn't enough to simply lead; sheep must be fed as they travel the course dictated by the vision. Sheep don't eat well when they feel insecure.

As pastors lead their congregations toward change, the people must be fed with the truths that create an understanding of the need for that change. People are asking, "Why are we doing this? Where are we going? How will this make me a better Christian? How will this increase my opportunities to serve the Lord?" Properly led and fed, they will follow.

THE 700/800 BARRIER

After breaking the 100/200 barrier, the next barrier to growth will occur at seven hundred to eight hundred active members. Our church had been stuck at about eight hundred for more than a year. We would pass the mark but then drop below it. I had heard there was a wall to growth around this point but arrogantly thought we could ignore it and just break right through; however, ignoring it was no longer possible.

Personally, it was taking its toll on me. It is amazing that as each barrier is approached, the senior pastor feels it first. This is because the greatest change will have to come in the senior pastor in order for growth to continue. Fortunately, pressure and stress are great motivators to increase knowledge! That is, in fact, one of the reasons for writing this book. I have a burden to help pastors anticipate and make the required adjustments before they hit "the wall."

I asked our administrator to order a workbook/manual on breaking the 700/800 barrier that I had spotted in a catalog. When it came, I was like a little kid and immediately began flipping through it on my way from the administration office into my office. I saw one diagram, closed the book, and never picked it up again. I knew exactly what to do. Breaking the 700/800 barrier follows the same dynamics as the 100/200 barrier, but on a macro scale.

As discussed earlier, to surpass one or two hundred active members, a church has to restructure from one swollen fellowship circle to multiple circles, allowing more space for people to connect with a pastor and with one another. It has everything to do with people making connections. But as circles increase, so do the management responsibilities of the senior leader. Consequently, the elders' meetings increase in length and frequency to keep up with all the ministry demands. Decisions simply have to be made.

Managing a church like this can be very cumbersome, and things tend to fall through the cracks. Planning can also be a

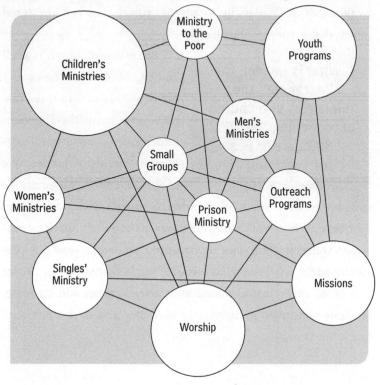

nightmare. One ministry, for instance, might schedule an event on the same night as another. Since the church is not small, neither are these groups, rendering last-minute changes nearly impossible, if not overwhelmingly unprofessional. As the previous diagram suggests, adding fellowship circles has allowed for more growth but creates a crisis of leadership that threatens to strangle the very growth it facilitated.

What is needed to "detangle" the ministries of a church approaching the 700/800 barrier is a restructuring of leadership to form circles of circles. Another layer of leadership must be established, this time among the paid staff, to whom new levels of authority and responsibility must be delegated. There are a variety of ways to do this. In a departmental church, circles may be grouped into macro departments, where a number of pastors work under the leadership of another pastor who is empowered to run that section of the church.

> **What is needed to "detangle" the ministries of a church approaching the 700/800 barrier is a restructuring of leadership.**

Because our church is a cell church, we divided the county the church is in into three districts and grouped cell groups under each according to categories—circles of circles. We placed a senior associate to oversee the daily affairs of the church, since my responsibilities outside the church (duties within our network of churches, missions, overseeing churches we had planted) had increased. As the church grew, we designated a fourth circle comprised of singles and youth cells. Just like medium-sized churches add circles to facilitate continued growth, large churches add circles of circles to do the same.

The 700/800 Barrier Diagram #1

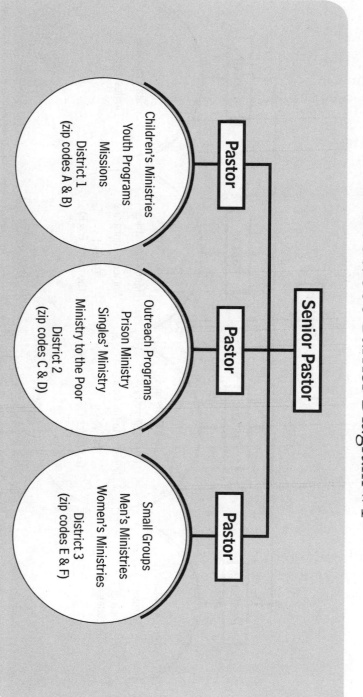

Senior Pastor

Pastor

Children's Ministries
Youth Programs
Missions
District 1
(zip codes A & B)

Pastor

Outreach Programs
Prison Ministry
Singles' Ministry
Ministry to the Poor
District 2
(zip codes C & D)

Pastor

Small Groups
Men's Ministries
Women's Ministries
District 3
(zip codes E & F)

The 700/800 Barrier Diagram #2 — With Youth and Singles

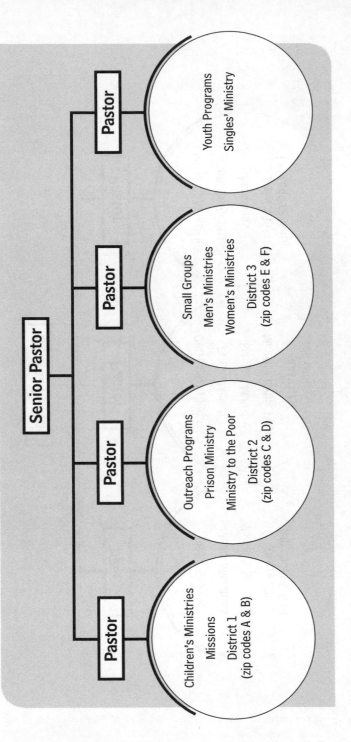

Senior Pastor

Pastor

Children's Ministries
Missions
District 1
(zip codes A & B)

Pastor

Outreach Programs
Prison Ministry
Ministry to the Poor
District 2
(zip codes C & D)

Pastor

Small Groups
Men's Ministries
Women's Ministries
District 3
(zip codes E & F)

Pastor

Youth Programs
Singles' Ministry

An Adjustment in the Elders

To overcome the 700/800 barrier, two other crucial adjustments had to be made. The elders first had to relinquish control of certain aspects of leadership to the staff. At the time, all of the district pastors were elders, but the five other pastors were not. If all the pastors are elders, then there really is no difference between an elder and a pastor in terms of the function of church government. The elders, at least the paid ones, would still have their hands in the daily operations of the church. The senior pastor would then be forced to decide between keeping the operations of government functioning like a medium-sized church or only having paid elders. First, there is a conflict of interest in the latter scenario. Second, there would be no functional elders governing the local church, only five-fold type leaders (see Ephesians 4:11). The New Testament clearly calls for elders in every church (see Acts 14:23).

An Adjustment in the Pastoral Staff

The second crucial adjustment needed was for the staff, particularly those at the district tier, to be empowered to lead at a new level. Each district was set up to function basically like a church within a church. (Just as the circles in the medium-sized church allow for more people to make connections, in the large church the grouping of circles under one leader allows for more circles to be created. When the management of a district gets to be too much for one district pastor, or when that district presses in on the eight-hundred-member barrier, simply create more districts.) The entire pastoral staff as a unit was also empowered to create a yearly calendar to facilitate the pursuit of the vision and create corresponding provisional budgets. Final approval of the budget is in the hands of the eldership, since their focus is on the big picture and not one district or aspect of church life.

Once all these pieces were in place and the church was gently led along, we sailed right past the eight-hundred mark. The momentum was awesome! I became even more passionate about the fact that infrastructure of the local church, particularly the relationship of the senior pastor and the other staff pastors to the eldership, is fundamental to breaking growth barriers.

THE KEY

The key to breaking both of these barriers is not so much how but why. There are hidden dynamics at work that must be appreciated and can be anticipated. Understanding them enables us to be creative in developing the mechanisms necessary to break through. All the principles are the same in each context; however, the outworking might be different. Things may look one way in one church and different in another, even though both applied the same principles.

> **At every level, barrier-breaking begins in the brain. First, the pastor must look ahead and anticipate that change is required.**

At every level, barrier-breaking begins in the brain. First, the pastor must look ahead and anticipate that change is required. Second, the pastor must imagine how the church at the next level should function and how it should be structured, and then he must lead the leadership team to see the same thing. Third, the pastor must begin to formulate a plan to rebuild the infrastructure of the church to fit the newly envisioned model. As the pastor and elders adjust their functioning relationship, growth will naturally occur. Finally, step by step, the congregation needs to be led and fed as changes are implemented.

Tension mounts as churches approach a growth barrier. In order to make the jump to the next level, certain internal operations must be adjusted beyond restructuring the leadership team. In the next chapter, I will give some practical suggestions on how to make the necessary changes to go over the top.

Tension Points Produced by Growth Barriers

CHAPTER FOUR

IT IS MUCH EASIER to pastor a church of four hundred active members than a church of two hundred. By the same token, leading a church of fifteen hundred is infinitely easier than leading a church of eight hundred. Numbers aren't really the issue. As I have said, the key to growing a church is the leader's ability to change the church's internal structures. Those internal changes primarily concern how the elders, senior pastor, and staff relate to one another, who does the ministry, and how decisions are made.

A church of two hundred active members arrived at that plateau by developing a certain methodology of ministry and a governmental infrastructure that fueled its growth. However, the methodology and infrastructure has run its course of usefulness. This didn't happen overnight. Gradually, the old methods and infrastructural design began failing to produce the same results as in the earlier days when the church was smaller. In fact, growth is being impeded. The same dynamic is at work in a church that has bumped up against the 700/800 wall.

THE DEVELOPING TENSION

Why is leading a church of three hundred members easier than a church of two hundred? Why is leading more than one thousand people easier than eight hundred? Tension. The barriers actually create tension and make leading and managing a church approaching or parked at a barrier more difficult to lead. Look again at the chart on page 48. Notice the line dividing the small church from the medium-sized church and the line dividing the medium-sized church from the large one. These lines are designated 100/200 and 700/800 respectively, indicating the presence of a church-growth barrier. The mechanisms employed to get a church *to* this threshold will never help it *across* it. In fact, the closer a church gets to a growth wall ahead, the more tension develops. And that tension is actually caused by the breakdown of the very mechanisms that once worked so effectively to get the church to this place.

As mentioned earlier, the elders in a small church "do" the ministry and make all the decisions. When the church is less than one hundred members, this makes for pleasant kingdom activity. But as a church approaches two hundred, there are more people to counsel, comfort, and correct. Decisions demand to be made, so elders' meetings creep past the time limit set in days when the church was a manageable one hundred.

Getting home late after meetings and other church functions increases tension in the home. Tension naturally increases as the number of people who require ministry exceeds the limits of those who minister. Older and less needy members feel neglected. New ministries must be created to keep up with the demand for more pastoral care and to maximize the opportunities presented by the gifting and interests of new and maturing people.

It is not uncommon for an elder or two to step down during this period. Feeling pressure at home, pressure at work, and pressure at church, they request a break. What does that do to the others on the eldership team? With the departure of the resting friend, the workload only increases. Elders sometimes begin to question the senior pastor's management style. ("Is it really necessary to meet for three hours every week? Perhaps you could do a little more by way of preparation for these meetings!") At times, stress surfaces between the elders. ("Do you really have to ask forty-five questions about every issue we face?")

A change in structure will change everything and take the small church over the very barrier that is causing the tension and has made life at two hundred miserable. Again, while the dynamics are different, tension caused by outdated structures is the reason for problems at seven to eight hundred members as well.

As was stated earlier, small, medium, and large churches are completely different from each other. A medium-sized church is not a small church with more members. Nor is a large church simply a medium-sized church with a greater attendance. All are churches, true, but it would be best to think of them as various species in one family. They are simply not the same. This is no small point, so let me emphasize it! Almost everything about a small church is different from a medium-sized church—the way they communicate, how they recruit volunteers, how they prepare for events, how they make decisions, how they get the worship center ready for the service. *Everything is different.* A medium-sized church is simply a different animal. The same holds true of the large church. To move from small to medium or from medium to large, some very important things will have to change! It is important, then, to understand the dynamics involved in a church at the next level in order to take a congregation to that place.

A church that has hit a growth barrier (100/200 or 700/800) has only three choices: (1) Divide the congregation into multiple congregations and plant new churches; (2) stay the way it is and plateau at this barrier (in most cases, the church will develop an oscillating pattern of slight growth and decline); or (3) change and move into the next phase of development. The key word is *change;* a local church cannot break through a growth barrier and remain the way it is. It must change.

Change is not an event. Change is a process. I have seen more than one zealous pastor, filled with a vision that is truly from God, turn the ship too quickly, spilling people over the side. The initiative designed to promote growth and build momentum actually hindered both. In such cases, unwise leaders and core members shake off the setback by decrying the lost congregants as those who didn't "want to go on with God." In reality, the loss is a result of leadership that was not patient and deliberate in introducing changes to the congregation. The larger the ship, the slower it turns. The church is no longer the little motorized skiff that once met in someone's living room. You cannot steer two hundred people the way you steered fifty. Turning a ship of eight hundred people the way you turned her at two hundred is a great way to "grow" the church to six hundred!

Few people readily and happily embrace change. Most, in fact, resist it. Over time, though, the majority of people will get on board. But if you wait for everyone to get in the game, the crowd will be gone before the starting whistle finally blows. Ignore the few who forever speak of the old days as better than the present. People who live in the past will likely never be won over. On the other hand, having people immediately accept a new initiative might deceive you into thinking that now is the time to aggressively advance. Some people love change; change is exciting in their view. For them, the future is now. But in the long run they aren't normally "builders."

The true builders in a church are the ones who represent a middle group—people who initially resist change but eventually get on board. These are the ones you have to reach in order for you to get where God has called. But how? Every leader navigating a church over a growth barrier needs to consider three issues: the problem, the paradigm, and the personnel. And each issue needs to be addressed on two levels: elders and people.

THE 100/200 BARRIER
1. The Problem: We have reached a barrier. We must change to keep growing.

A. The Elders

It won't take much to convince the elders that change is needed. They have been living with a growing tension for some time prior to reaching the wall of one to two hundred members. It is the reason for change, but it is also the type of change that they are likely to resist.

The idea that growth barriers exist is not in the Bible. No Sunday school curriculum that I know of ever mentions them. And, unfortunately, most pastors have never educated the leaders on the topic. Consequently, the idea has never been batted around in an elders' meeting. The elders must be instructed. Expose the leaders to some writings by C. Peter Wagner. Dare I suggest . . . distribute this book among them and discuss it together? Do whatever you have to do, but educate the elders in advance of initiating any change.

In addition to the fact that most people want to be wanted, the power and prestige of being the conduits through whom all decisions and ministry flows is intoxicating. The change you are calling for, as indicated by the chart on page 48, is for the elders to include others in the flow of ministry, delegating responsibility and the corresponding authority. Many are threatened by this and will resist at first. Wise pastors must help elders see that they are not being replaced. They are, in fact, being taken "up" not "down" since they will actually be "over" those doing the ministry.

B. The People

The average member does not care in the least about church-growth barriers. Whole sermons on the subject are not likely to be met with enthusiasm. In fact, I have found, sadly, that most people are not convinced the church needs to grow. Therefore, any call for sacrifice to facilitate growth will probably be resisted. Instead, the pastor should concentrate on creating an understanding that the church *should* grow, and further, that its growth will *actually benefit* the average believer! C. Peter Wagner's *Leading Your Church to Growth* (Regal Books) and *Your Church Can Grow* (Regal Books) and Gary McIntosh's *Biblical Church Growth* (Baker Books) are wonderful resources and contain loads of great material for constructing messages that will speak to this issue.

Above all, seek to destroy all nongrowth thinking. Get it out of the church and stand guard at the door so it can never creep back in. Why? Because growing a church is never about simply increasing numbers. Growing a church is about emptying hell and filling up heaven. It is about making room for harvest and harvesters alike. Who would turn someone away from the table of life? By camping on the underside of a growth barrier, churches passively reject displaced believers and the lost every day.

I remember a time when our church was busting at the seams and it was evident that a new building was needed. The inconvenience of patrolling the parking lot for a spot and standing through services hoping to find a seat was causing folks' patience to wear thin. These people had embraced growth and were enthusiastic proponents of our aggressive evangelistic thrust, but I sensed it was time for another dose of kingdom reality. In a sermon I brought up the thought that no one would dare put into words. I hypothetically proposed, with no small hint of sarcasm, that perhaps we had grown enough; perhaps we should plan to taper off. I suggested putting a sign on the door telling newcomers that we didn't want them. If they were believers, we were only depriving them of fellowship, a fellowship we enjoy. For unbelievers, I proposed it would be more accurate to post a sign that simply said, "Go to hell!" since we were depriving them of a chance to hear the gospel and come to Christ for salvation.

I also pointed out that we already had too many people, so we would actually need to empty some of our services of the folks who were already in our midst. After all, if the church has become too big, then some obviously need to go! I suggested appointing a committee to get rid of people we didn't like. "But what happens if you're chosen to leave?" I asked. "Would you still feel the church was too big?"

> **Growing a church is never about simply increasing numbers. Growing a church is about emptying hell and filling up heaven. It is about making room for harvest and harvesters alike.**

To keep the story in context, we were experiencing extreme conditions, and these folks had been under fifteen years of teaching on why it was best for them that the church continued to grow. By the time the ruse was up, and everyone in the place could see the obvious, we had to do whatever was necessary to make room for all those whom God would bring our way. We built the building without debt.

2. The Paradigm: The role of the elders must change.

A. The Elders

As we have established, for a church to pass the 100/200 mark, the internal relationship of elders to ministry must undergo adjustment. First, the elders need to recognize that in letting go of ministry, they are not letting go of their role or authority in the church. The chief function of the eldership is to rule, and the calling on every believer is to minister. Elders aren't losing anything in releasing ministry and an appropriate amount of authority over that ministry. Their role is the same—to rule over. In fact, their role has increased, since what they have rule over has increased.

Second, elders must resist the temptation to micromanage. As noted earlier, in the small church, elders make all the decisions. Now they must allow for some decisions to be made at the ministry level. Certainly there are limits, but elders must empower people to lead in their designated spheres of responsibility.

An illustration here is in order. A new director of children's ministries will likely need more guidance than one who has been performing the function for years. The new director might, for instance, need help in choosing curriculum. In fact, the elders may decide to select it. But in the case of a person who has years of experience, he or she may be given the authority to change curriculum and even set the annual children's budget. Someone with years of experience but little wisdom or lots of "attitude," on the other hand, may be very limited in the types of decisions he or she is allowed to make.

The idea of delegating responsibility and authority is organic and unique to each church situation; but the point is, in order for a church to grow and people to mature, elders must shift from doing ministry to being over ministry—from being hands-on to hands-in.

B. The People

When a church is smaller, the pastor is looking for volunteers. In a medium-sized church, the pastor is looking for leaders. There is simply too much for the elders to do; other leaders must come forward. I have often heard pastors say they lack leaders in their congregations. I believe the real problem is not a lack of leadership but a lack of perception on the part of the pastor. I heard Tommy Barnett, pastor of the huge First Assembly of God in Phoenix, Arizona, once say, "All you need to reach your city is already in your house [church]." That statement changed my life. Rather than waiting for God to bring great people to our church, I began to look for great people already in the congregation.

Some say leaders are born, not made. No matter what you read on leadership, let me emphatically state that most leaders are made, not born. Leaders "become"; they don't appear. In fact, the best leaders are the ones you raise up yourself, right in the house— not the ones who come to you from the outside. The leaders trained from within hold your values as nonnegotiable. Your philosophy of ministry is already inculcated into the fabric of their leadership style. They love and follow you because you brought them into their destiny. Leaders brought in from the outside have to be engrafted into the vision of the house and trained in your values and philosophy of ministry before they can be fully released.

"But he [or she] isn't ready!" I have heard pastor after pastor (all with churches under two hundred members) make that statement about a potential leader. The truth is, no one is truly ready for the next step in life. You weren't ready for marriage. You thought you were until the first big blow up. You weren't ready for children, although you thought you knew everything about kids. You judged all your friends who had kids as failures until you had a couple of children. You weren't ready for ministry either, although as a senior in Bible college or in seminary you just "knew" the church you planted would break one thousand in the first few years. No one is ready! So what are you waiting for? Put people in ministry! Don't be foolish or hasty, but look at people through the eyes of faith.

I have appointed thousands of leaders over the years, but I have seldom heard others applaud my choice with "he is the man [or woman]!" Instead, the vast majority of my choices have been made in the face of mild opposition. "Can she really do it?" "I'm not sure about him." "She isn't ready." "You might be setting him up for failure." Interestingly, leaders who weren't universally supported themselves at first have often been among those voicing opposition to new ones coming along.

Believe in others more than they believe in themselves and you will always be successful. Those you raise up will propel you to success.

3. The Personnel: We must move from the Shepherd Model to the Rancher Model.

A. The Elders

Elders are the example-setters in the church; people naturally look to them since they are leaders. As noted earlier, for a church to break the 100/200 barrier, it must switch from the Shepherd Model to the Rancher Model. A second full-time pastor must be brought on staff, or at least (as a temporary measure) an elder functioning as an associate must be raised up. This "second" can't just be a good person who is cheap (inexpensive to hire) and happens to be at hand. This person has to be the kind of leader to whom people can go as a "the-buck-stops-here" person— someone who can make a final decision. When this leader makes a hospital visit, the member feels visited and is not looking for the senior pastor to come. When this leader counsels, folks are satisfied that they have been competently counseled.

Obviously, it is imperative that people have confidence in this "second" if the church is to go forward. Elders need to take the lead in this, intentionally getting behind the associate and following that person as they would the senior pastor. How elders respond to this leader will dictate how the people will respond.

B. The People

I suppose the most foolish thing a senior pastor could do in shifting from the Shepherd Model to the Rancher Model is to ask the people who the next staff member should be. A vote on this issue is a promise of divided loyalty. A pastor can't herd people over the 100/200 barrier—they must be led. As the pastor must prepare the people for change and make room for growth, so the pastor must prepare them to receive the next staff member. In advance of hiring a new person, tell the people there is a new person coming. Describe the position and tactfully tell the people how you see them relating to the person filling the new position. As you outline the job description, explain how you, as senior pastor, will also follow this new person in the areas in which you delegate responsibility.

I am not in any way advocating co-equal pastoral authority in the church. But when the one who is "over" is secure enough to come "under" in certain areas, it pushes up the subordinate in the eyes of the people to new levels of respect, establishing the subordinate's authority in the house, thus making the whole church stronger. I would never bring this person into the position gradually, hoping the people will embrace the new associate pastor. This screams that you lack confidence either in the person or in the process of breaking the 100/200 barrier. Either way, you lose. Do your homework. Win the elders' wholehearted support. Prepare the people. Bring on the associate pastor. Shift to the Rancher Model. Break this barrier!

THE 700/800 BARRIER
1. The Problem: We have reached a barrier. We must change to keep growing.

A. The Elders

At the 100/200 level, the elders are among the first to experience tension as that barrier is approached. At the 700/800 mark, the pastor first, and then the pastoral staff, feels the pressure. The elders are likely unaware that this barrier even exists. Pastor and staff feel pressure because of the amount of effort required to manage a church with a multitude of ministries that have been generated over time to keep up with the needs of a diverse and growing congregation and to facilitate outreach into the community and the world. Phones ring nonstop, counseling piles up, and meetings run into other meetings. But the greatest creator of tension at this level is the realization that things are falling through the cracks.

The management style of simply adding more circles to

increase ministry has become unmanageable (see chapter 3). The pastor is no longer free to be a leader but instead has become a manager of what has been built, and he may not be a very good manager at that. The pastor feels like the guy on the *Ed Sullivan Show* (showing my age) who used to spin numerous plates on poles. As the spinner added plate after plate, excitement built as the audience waited for a plate to drop. It makes for a great show, but a tough life. Eventually, a plate or two does hit the ground. On the *Ed Sullivan Show*, the plates were porcelain; in the church, the plates are people.

If elders notice anything, it is that their meetings seem to run longer and longer, and completing an entire agenda is rare. There is a reason for this. In a medium-sized church, elders make ministry decisions. These decisions are carried out in the daily life of the church. By the time a church reaches seven or eight hundred members, there are a number of pastors on staff, all leading sections of the church and all needing decisions to be made in order to carry on the ministry. Since those decisions are made primarily by the elders, the hands of the pastors are effectively tied as they wait for decisions to be made. Agendas, therefore, get longer and longer. Elders who have been in that position since the 100/200 days may feel they have returned to the old days.

Sometimes elders chafe under the weight of the growing number of decisions they face, especially since they feel more and more distant from the actual function of ministry. They may feel they need more information to make good decisions—information not always readily given since meeting time is limited and decisions demand to be made. Clearly, the elders' role in making decisions regarding the daily operation of the church, and the alignment of the staff in relation to ministry, needs to be revisited in order for this tension to be eased. Mounting tension of this type signals the approach of a barrier to growth.

B. The People

Much like the 100/200 barrier, members of a church approaching the 700/800 mark feel like they are getting less ministry and attention than they did formerly. While each pastor on staff has areas of responsibility, the "taking care of people" part is largely determined by the people, whose propensity is to receive from their pastor of choice. Someone working in children's ministry may like the way the youth pastor counsels and go to that pastor for help. Another, serving on the worship team, runs into financial trouble and seeks help from the outreach pastor, since that pastor handles money well.

> When pastors become managers *of* ministry instead of equippers *for* ministry, growth potential is inhibited.

Managing ministries, being available to leaders, and connecting with people according to their whim is fine when the church is at five hundred members or so, but at seven or eight hundred a new management style is needed that is somewhat more directive for the people. Remember, releasing more people into ministry will keep the church in its pattern of growth. But when pastors become managers *of* ministry instead of equippers *for* ministry, growth potential is inhibited and people fall through the cracks.

2. The Paradigm: The roles of pastors and elders must change.

A. The Elders

The following represents the most difficult shift for elders to make, but it is vital that it occurs if the church is going to break the 700/800 barrier. Two simultaneous processes must take place. First, the elders must move from being decision-makers to becoming policy-makers. Second, the circles of ministry (diagrammed in chapter 3) must be regrouped into circles of circles, and the pastoral configuration must be realigned to facilitate this. We'll look at each in turn.

Policies govern decisions. Policies are decisions themselves, but at a macro or philosophical level. Policies are like railroad tracks. Someone at the executive level in the railroad company decided where they would provide service and what type of business they were looking for. They would haul logs or cattle. They would service automakers or shipyards. In the end, these philosophical discussions led to the laying of track. After the tracks were in place, engineers would decide how many cars to connect to a given engine. Further, the conductor would make decisions concerning the schedule. Another person would decide the menu for the dining car of a passenger train and shop accordingly. It is clear that the policies made at the executive level dictated the type of service provided and where. After that, thousands of smaller decisions were made daily by the people actually running the train to provide quality rail service. It would be absurd, for example, to think the railroad executives would meet daily to decide the next day's menu.

Elders in a church beyond eight hundred active members must become policy-makers. They lay track for the pastors to follow and release them to make the daily decisions in order to provide "quality rail service."

In the church under eight hundred, elders make ministry decisions and are over ministry. In the church beyond eight hundred, elders make policy decisions; *the staff is over ministry*, making decisions collectively at times, much like an eldership in a medium-sized church.

In order to circumvent the growing confusion caused by the multiplication of ministry circles (see page 63), a church only has two choices: (1) Stop adding new ministries and bring growth to a halt, or (2) reconfigure pastoral alignment. As I mentioned in chapter 3, this reconfiguration requires restructuring circles of ministry into circles of circles. There is no set way to design these circles of circles, since the style and function of each church will dictate how these structures are built. A departmental church will be organized differently than a cell-based church. A departmental church that is a teaching center will be configured differently than a departmental church whose philosophy of ministry is outreach-oriented.

You may want to review the diagrams on pages 65–66, but the point here is to see the big picture and build a paradigm to fit your church's style and function. Think in terms of groupings, but always keep in mind that releasing people into ministry is our main job. In the long run this is what provides growth, because this is what matures people. Structures either inhibit or promote this process. When the structures that used to release people now inhibit that flow, they must be changed. Look for where people fall through the cracks. Look for places where two pastors cover the same ground. Look for natural lines of demarcation.

Some churches build their groupings departmentally—all education in circle A, for example. Under that might be children's ministries, adult Sunday school, home groups (in a teaching-oriented church), etc. Perhaps outreach would fall under category B, including such things as visitation, greeters, evangelism, home groups (in an evangelistically oriented church), etc. Pastoral care might be under category C, covering the areas of singles, youth, counseling, etc. I mentioned earlier that our church is a cell church. Some cell churches break up their communities into geographic districts and place their people and cells under pastors by zip code or neighborhoods. Others organize their cells into categories, much like a departmental church, and group types of cells by category under various pastors. The easiest way to build circles of circles is to follow the natural lines of organization.

B. The People

It will take some adjustment on the part of the people to get used to doing things a new way. Life in a church of eight hundred people is simply different than one of five hundred. Fellowship, discipleship, evangelism, worship, etc. are basically the same, but the way in which these occur is different at the higher-number level. The clearest example of how things have changed is in the area of communication. In most medium-sized churches, while pastors have specific job descriptions, the people get used to going to their favorite source for counsel and information. They simply expect all the pastors to be up on everything going on in the church: "Ya'll work there [our church is in the South] all together, so I just figured you'd know what was goin' on."

In a church of over eight hundred, structures and the lines of communication that support them must become clearer. While this is a hassle to those used to church life another way, it is for their benefit that these changes are made. Sending members to the right people allows for a higher quality product. A larger church requires a higher degree of specialization from its pastors. This means if you talk to a pastor serving in district one, that pastor may have no clue about what is happening in district two, but can answer anything you ask about district one. People get better service, and they are better known and cared for as specialization increases. Fewer people fall by the wayside.

3. The Personnel: We must create another tier of pastoral leadership in the church.

A. The Elders

"What's wrong with the way we have it configured now? It seems to be working." Of course, that is what most elders will feel since the 700/800 barrier is tougher on the pastoral staff than it is on the eldership. (The 100/200 mark specifically pinches elders.) The elders need to see that there must be a realignment that will, by necessity, change the way the pastors relate to the eldership and to one another. In a medium-sized church, all the pastors, with the exception of the senior pastor, are likely to be on the same level. While they all perform different jobs, they all relate as subordinates to one person, the senior pastor.

When a church realigns the circles of ministry into circles of circles, some pastors will wind up over others on the organizational chart. This is necessary for two reasons: (1) The senior pastor can return to functioning as a leader instead of a manager, since the management responsibilities belong to the new tier of leaders on the "district" or larger "department" level; and (2) creating a new level of leadership will focus the responsibilities of those leaders into clearly defined areas, increasing accountability, closing cracks, and providing more opportunity for people to be released into ministry.

To effectively run a district or mega-department, a leader will have to "bring up" new leaders into ministry. Suppose a baseball team divided into three squads. Before, the single team had one shortstop, one first baseman, one catcher, etc. Now that the team is three squads, three shortstops are needed, three first basemen, three catchers, etc.

How do we decide who the new "district pastors" or "departmental pastors" will be? Remember, in realigning the staff this way, you have created another level of leadership; therefore, these positions must be filled by people who are leaders. I like to think of the folks who fill these slots as people who could be senior pastors themselves. They may not be gatherers in the sense that they have the gift to take a church to this level, but they need to be people who are capable of leading/managing a large and growing number of people. As the church continues to grow, pastors on this tier will be responsible for hundreds (possibly thousands) of people, as well as a number of pastors working under them. The wrong leader, one who does not have the capacity to operate at this level, could hinder growth.

It is possible that in realigning, new positions may have to be created and new pastors brought on staff to fill these slots. In our case, we were not in a position to hire these folks right away. We added the positions to the organizational chart and temporarily penciled in existing pastors into more than one slot. These pastors were required for a time to wear more than one hat. Recognizing that these infrastructural changes would produce growth, and therefore an increase in finances, we established a priority list for hiring new pastors and support personnel. As funds were available, we brought on the required individuals.

B. The People

How you communicate these changes to the congregation is crucial. Shared the wrong way, the people are likely to feel they are losing their pastor and being shuffled off to some low-grade associate. Again, if people are led and fed, they will follow a leader anywhere. I had these two principles in mind when I first told the congregation of the shifts we were making.

Before I addressed the specific (and quite radical) adjustments, I tried to firmly establish in the people's minds that we were growing, and that growth was a good thing. Then I assured them that in the future, they would continue to be fed. "As you know, we are growing. And since we are committed to providing quality pastoral care for you and your family, we are going to make some changes. As we grow, we don't want pastoral care to get farther away from you. As it stands right now, it is harder and harder to get to me. I have to make appointments with myself! We want pastoral care to be closer and more accessible to you." You can see that these words speak to the issue of feeding; sheep want to be cared for. They need shepherding. That's why we need to restructure—so members can connect with a shepherd.

Not only must sheep be fed, they must be led. I presented the manner in which we had devised a provision for more effective pastoral care. "As of November first, we are dividing the county into three districts and establishing a district pastor over each. Each person, therefore, as of that day, will have a personal pastor. Whereas it has been increasingly difficult to get to me, it is the job of these pastors to be available to you. They will marry your children and bury your parents. They will visit you in the hospital and counsel you as needed.

"I, on the other hand, will no longer do pastoral counseling. My role will be to lead the church into all God has called us to and do my very best to empower these pastors to be the best they can be in serving you and releasing you into the ministry to which you have been called." I further outlined the new configuration, detailing how these changes would provide greater opportunity for all to come into maturity by being released into greater levels of ministry. The new changes were enthusiastically embraced and growth resulted. The barrier was broken.

It is easier to start something than it is to maintain it! Members and staff must be trained to function in a new paradigm. For instance, when people called the office looking for a pastor with whom they could talk, our staff was trained to ask, "Do you know who your district pastor is?" If the caller did not, each staff member was equipped with a card outlining the zip codes of each district. Budgets were drafted and monies were spent along district lines. Our districts operated almost like three churches within one church, so each person on staff had to be trained to think in terms of districts, not just Manna Church. Over time, both staff and congregation got it. But even now, we are training new members and sometimes reminding old ones how to relate in a life-giving way to our structure.

The chart on page 48 breaks churches into three size categories. In each category, the infrastructure of the church functions differently from the others. What happens when an elder or pastor is functioning according to the wrong size category? What if multiple leaders are functioning in different size categories? Tension develops along two lines. First, tension points are produced by growth barriers, which has been the subject of this chapter. Second, the most damaging and most severe tension is caused by the improper alignment of pastors and elders in reference to their church size. This is the topic of the next chapter.

Tension Produced by Improper Alignment

UNFORTUNATELY, I HAVE SEEN the following scenario too many times. And routinely, when I discuss it in pastors' groups, attendees roll their eyes. The all too familiar scene takes place whenever elders' meetings are held in a church that has begun to approach the 100/200 barrier. As described in the last chapter, tension builds as the church draws near this first major growth roadblock. As the elders' discussion turns to what it will take to go to the next level, invariably, the pastor and an elder or two are already there. They recognize the need to change internal operations and hire staff. But the rub is exactly how and who?

As the meeting grinds on and opinions are expressed, there is often one voice that undercuts the whole process and takes the church back to the "dark ages," leaving her stuck under the shadow of the seemingly impenetrable two-hundred-member wall. Whenever this voice expresses itself, it usually wins the day. I can hear it now. One leader sits quietly, listening to the discussion on the present state of affairs in the church and finally speaks: "Brothers, do you remember the days when things were so much easier? Remember when we gathered as friends in Pastor Jim's living room? We would talk and pray and just let the Holy Spirit lead us. We did the work together and loved it. Now look at us. We meet in a conference room and talk church business the whole time. We are so busy and so pressured. Brothers, we need to get back to the old days. Remember when Brother [so and so did such and such] . . . ?" Every one laughs, bitten by the nostalgia bug, fogging the brain and intoxicating the heart with memories of days when life seemed better.

At this point, the pastor and the one forward-looking elder feel the moment, the meeting, and the momentum slipping away. While everyone else considers "how we got here—in this mess," the pastor tries to convince all that "how we got here" is the right question but to view it as an opportunity! Even so, the pastor will likely lose the day. He will go home, frustrated, and on the way call the one forward-looking elder on his cell phone.

These are the kinds of situations that cause pastors to want to give up, and in fact, many do. The numbers on pastoral burnout, depression, and departure from ministry in America today are staggering. Elders also suffer. These folks work secular jobs and serve in the church as a means of serving the Lord. Most have never been to a Bible college or seminary or served in full-time ministry. Most are too busy to keep up with all the current literature on how to lead or grow a church. They even find it difficult to keep up with all that is going on in their own congregations. They are simply the "best" people in the church—they serve, tithe, volunteer, support, and sacrifice without asking for praise or recognition.

In a situation like this, neither the pastor nor the elders realize what is happening. They all have great hearts and are doing their best to move the church forward and honor the Lord. All of them already feel the pressure produced by a barrier they probably don't know exists. And now, an even more damaging pressure has surfaced, robbing their unity and potentially destroying their relationships. The trouble is simple. The pastor and one elder see what needs to be done and intuitively respond to the present condition of the church by suggesting change. Others are still in a small-church mind-set and simply cannot see how change will help.

The real difficulty here, however, is not that everyone left the elders' meeting without a plan. It is that they left divided, not over the issue but in their thinking and in relation to one another, to ministry, and to how decisions should be made. The pastor and one elder are in medium-sized mode while the rest of the eldership is in small. The greatest tension is yet to come.

In fact, the most severe and potentially damaging tensions are those caused by pastors and individuals on the leadership team who relate to the church according to the wrong size category. This is one of the main reasons I am called in to help local churches. I see these

> **The most severe and potentially damaging tensions are those caused by pastors and individuals on the leadership team who relate to the church according to the wrong size category.**

types of improper alignment in all manner of situations. There is the one elder in a large church who still has a small-church mindset and carries the expectations associated with the small church. This elder wants to handle matters that should no longer be controlled at the eldership level.

I have also seen local churches led by a pastor with a large-church mindset in a small-church context. Having a vision to be a large church is great, but you can't skip the stages necessary to get there. In the pastor's impatience, structures have been implemented prematurely that tax the leadership team and cause the people to feel, in effect, "unpastored." In many situations, the pastor and individuals on the leadership team are all over the chart on page 48. It is no wonder that tensions result when they try to make decisions or do ministry together!

I have heard some of the most hurtful things said by the best of people, each suspicious of the other's motive and yet each with a heart burning for the church to experience God's best. Confused about the roles of both pastor and elders in the church, uncertain of how decisions are to be made and where the lines of authority are to be drawn, gridlock develops and, like a partisan Congress, great people take sides. Relationships suffer, unity is broken, church politics develop, and momentum for growth is lost. How can we avoid such a calamity?

1. EDUCATION PRODUCES LIBERATION

Simply put, the truth sets people free. Both pastor and elders need to recognize where they really are in the growth and life of the church. Often when I go over "the chart" with pastors and their eldership team, the result is confession and reconciliation. Honest discussion develops when people recognize what is happening.

Frequently, local churches do not have accurate records of where their membership is numerically. In such cases, the senior pastor guesses and sees three hundred, while the negative elder, who calls himself a realist, sees one hundred fifty. If the truth be told, both are probably wrong. How can they hope to lead the church properly if they have no honest appraisal of where they are? Decide on what an active member is and count worshipers each week. Keep good records and measure trends.

I have heard all kinds of objections to counting over the years. "God will judge the church if you count." The context for this idea is drawn from David's ill-fated effort to determine the military strength of Israel. His count amounted to a passive rejection of God as their Commander-in-Chief, the One who formerly fought for them. If your motive for counting is to establish your own importance in comparison to the other nations (local churches in your city), then you need to repent. If counting is a sin, then God is guilty. He counted the men of war in Israel, the number who died in various plagues, the 12 disciples, the 70, and the 120 in the Upper Room. He claimed 500 saw His Son alive after His death. He counted the people who responded to Peter's in-your-face altar calls in the early chapters of Acts. He even counts the number of hairs on our head! I think He is okay if we choose to count the number of people who attend our service, in an effort to find a reliable yardstick to measure the effectiveness of our service to Him.

Once a clear understanding of "how many we are" is developed, we need to come into agreement as to where the church is located on the chart; is it a small-, medium-, or large-sized church? Be careful to consider not just the numbers, but the mechanisms by which ministry is done and decisions are made.

Review the roles of pastors and elders as described earlier in this book. Talk about expectations. What are reasonable expectations that elders might have about their senior pastor and his God-given role in the local church? Is he making the vision clear? Do the elders fear his growing authority as the church expands? What are reasonable expectations that the senior pastor might have about the role of the elders in the local church? Are they releasing ministry and authority to others or holding on in an unhealthy way?

Talk about barriers and the need to change in order to break through the one you face. What specific changes need to occur now? Are you behind, ahead of the game, or right on time? What are the next steps?

Because most people, even leaders, naturally resist change, talk with your leadership team about the need for change in general. Establish the idea that the church is a living thing following a living God, so change will always be a part of a congregation's life. All living things experience change. Dead things don't really change; they just decay.

It sounds counterintuitive, but the senior pastor and leadership team need to review the vision of the church regularly. The pressures of life, including church life, can steal your focus away from the big picture of the mission God has for your specific local church. It's easy for church leaders and the senior pastor, the main visionary, to get bogged down in "stuff" and lose track of God's direction. In an effort to reeducate more than educate, it is a helpful exercise to talk again about why you exist as a church. Further, I would suggest setting some reasonable, measurable goals and reviewing them at least semiannually. These goals will help keep the church and its leadership on track.

> **The church is a living thing following a living God, so change will always be a part of a congregation's life.**

Finally, you simply can't talk enough about why the church should grow—why it has to grow. Make it a priority to talk frequently about growth with the staff as well as in the wider circles of leadership in the church, and preach and teach it from the pulpit.

2. COMMUNICATION PRODUCES COOPERATION

In all likelihood, there will be pastors or elders on the team who are not operating or thinking in the right context (a small-church-minded elder in a medium-sized church, a large-church-minded pastor in a one-hundred-member setting, etc.). The trouble is that most people do not see themselves accurately. A finger-pointing and I-told-you-so session is only going to hurt feelings and damage relationships.

In order to mature, we are instructed by Scripture to speak the truth in love to one another (Ephesians 4:15). Love in this setting demands that we take the non-confrontational approach. A generic discussion of how things ought to be done, how ministry is to be conducted, and how decisions are made at the church's stage development will create an atmosphere where the group can decide what the future will look like. In embracing the future and agreeing on how the pastor/elder team will relate, the members of the group are, in effect, turning from the past. I am not advocating ignoring the scriptural admonitions to clear offenses. I firmly believe that unforgiveness, bitterness, and resentment must be dealt with in a biblical manner, but never in a group context.

Each church is unique and has its own personality. Exactly how the individuals work together must be determined by the group itself. In the same way, who is over what and who answers to whom is very organic. There is no way this or any book can specifically outline the particulars of these dynamics in a given setting. But once a leadership team has accurately defined where the church is and openly communicated how they will relate both now and in the future, a spirit of cooperation is established. They may not be meeting any longer in Pastor Jim's living room, but the same life is now fueling the meetings once again. Unity is the order of the day, and momentum is recovered. Best of all, their relationships are mended and strong again. If the infrastructure, the bones of the church, is healthy, the rest of the body can grow. Communication produces cooperation.

3. EXPECTATION IS INVITATION

The most powerful byproduct of being on the same page is found in the idea that expectation produces invitation. Once you know where you are, you are able to see where you are going. With those two items in place, the visionaries go to work, devising a plan to take the church to the next level. Remembering the ideas about bringing a vision to pass (as discussed in chapter 1), the elders and pastors are able to create a plan to facilitate that vision, with specific reference to where the church is today. The exciting thing about this is that all involved recognize they are not dealing with a pipe dream but a real vision with teeth. This plan is based on facts—facts all parties have agreed upon.

Visions are brought to pass on the strength of unity, as Nehemiah's "Threefold Law of Vision" dictates (chapter 1). People work for what they own, and the best way to lead people toward owning a plan is to enlist them in developing it. Even though the plan may be long term, a church at three hundred fifty members outlines the steps to move toward seven hundred, for example. Elders and pastors alike are confident since they can see the end and the steps to get there. If the plan needs adjustment along the way, the team has the tools in hand to measure growth and address needs as they arise.

One of the important things a leadership team can expect is the approach of a new barrier and its inherent tension. If they can recognize that dynamic ahead of time, they will be able to implement change in stages as they draw nearer to the anticipated barrier. Discussions can be held well in advance of the roadblock and strategies developed to move them right through.

In discussing the 100/200 barrier, I heard C. Peter Wagner quote one of his students, Rick Warren, the now famous pastor of the giant Saddleback Community Church, as saying, "The best

way to break the two-hundred barrier is to never stop for it."
Assess where you are. Communicate with the team. Get everyone
on the same page and develop a plan. Use this plan as a tool—a
device to guide toward growth—anticipating tension and overcoming barriers.

When I meet with a group of pastors or with leaders in a local
church, a host of questions always follows the seminar, the most
common of which will be answered in the next chapter.

"So, What About . . . ?"
(Frequently Asked Questions)

CHAPTER SIX

AT THE END OF EVERY seminar with pastors or "strategy talk" with pastors and local church leaders, an ad hoc question-and-answer session follows. No two sessions are the same, since each is tailored to the dynamics of a particular church or group of churches. Three topics, however, phrased in terms of specific questions are common.

1. "WHO SHOULD I BRING ON STAFF TO HELP BREAK THE NEXT BARRIER?"

This question is almost always asked by leaders of churches under the two-hundred-member mark, and is often framed another way: "I have this really great youth guy [or music guy, or retired guy, or 'something' guy] who works for us part time.

Maybe I should just make him full time, and he will help us break this barrier."

These pastors may have unspoken promises concerning future employment that they are trying to avoid breaking. Perhaps they see an inexpensive way to accomplish their barrier-breaking goal. Or maybe they are just looking for the fastest way over the wall. But it is here that pastors should slow down and back up, because this is by far the most important hire they'll ever make. This decision will determine whether the church will break the 100/200 barrier or not.

Just because someone is a really great guy does not mean he should become "Number Two" in the transition from the Shepherd Model to the Rancher Model. As has already been said, this person needs to be someone who church members see in an authoritative/pastoral role—as a shepherd. Maybe the worship leader is that person. Maybe the youth leader is that person. But one thing is for sure. He isn't that person simply because he appears to be next in line by virtue of longevity or the fact that he presently occupies a part-time staff position.

This is the point where a good number of churches make the mistake that will forever keep them on the small side of the 100/200 barrier. At one hundred eighty members or so, most churches only have the funds to pay one other full-time pastor. Often, as soon as they reach this mark, numerically or financially, they run right out and "buy" themselves one of the two traditional first hires—a music person or a youth person. If they are fortunate, they have hired an individual who can also fill the shoes of a shepherd to the church. Most often, though, they get what they bought—a really great music leader or a young person who is loved by youth and parents alike, and not a second shepherd-type pastor.

My advice? It is always better to have a "jack-of-all-trades and master of none" as your second full-time pastor and use volunteers for youth and worship until you break the two-hundred-member barrier, that is, unless the youth or worship person has the ability to serve both in his specialized ministry and wear the shepherd's hat as well.

"So how can I tell if my youth guy has that capacity?" You cannot measure this according to an individual's desire or your vision for his or her life. You can always tell someone is a leader by considering these questions: Do people outside the scope of the individual's ministry follow him or her? Are people in the church, though not directly under the person, attracted to him or her? Do they seek that person out? Does this individual possess the "power of convocation" (the ability to gather people)? Watch the person in question before and after services; do people naturally gravitate toward him or her? Are the groups he or she leads among the largest or most successful in the church? Can this person easily attract volunteers? If the answers are yes, you have a leader on your hands. Hire away! If not, leave that person in his or her present position and allow the person time to develop without the pressure of being expected to provide what he or she cannot yet give.

2. "WHAT DO I DO WITH AN ELDER WHO CANNOT 'MAKE THE JUMP' TO THE NEXT LEVEL?"

This question has to be answered on several levels.

First, this situation is always going to be present in a growing church. As a church develops and moves from one level to the next, people adapt to change and to changing structures at different rates. The ease of personal adaptation is not determined by a person's intelligence or commitment to a vision, but rather by the person's temperament and personality, which have been provided by God. As leaders, we are required by God to provide an environment where people can embrace change and work through the ramifications associated with that change in their own souls. Sometimes it is just a matter of giving leaders the necessary time to make these internal adjustments, in which case the senior pastor should be patient, though not passive. Give the leaders time, but continue to gently educate the elder(s) in question concerning what is needed for the church to move on to the next level.

> **As a church develops and moves from one level to the next, people adapt to change and to changing structures at different rates.**

Second, it should be noted that without pressure, everything naturally reverts to form. Pastors sometimes labor through the process of determining that change is necessary—building a consensus among the elders toward that end—only to abandon the process once a conclusion has been made, falsely assuming that everyone is forever on board. When one or more elders "revert to form" in the following week's board meeting and function in the old way of thinking, the visionary leader, who long ago moved to the next level in his mind, cannot believe his ears. Mutiny! "Where were these people last week? Didn't they hear anything we said?" Of course they did, but in both the short and long runs, the growth process will have to be revisited and leaders reminded that they all agreed to operate in a different paradigm, and why this is good for all. Leading is our job. It is a process.

Third, there are those who seem incapable or unwilling to change the way they function. These people have built a wall around what "is" as if it will always be, and refuse to recognize that their "is" has become a "was." Amazingly, they are oblivious to the fact that others have moved on. It's okay for church members to be this way, but church leaders who refuse to grow and change with the group become roadblocks and they must be repositioned. Of course, any repositioning of a leader must be done in accordance with the by-laws that govern that local church or denomination.

Caution! How you approach a roadblock at the leadership level is a statement of the type of leader you are. Many un-principled leaders simply remove these people from their positions and discard them like some disposable product whose expiration date has passed. For leaders like this, the forward progress of the organization is the highest value they hold. Please remember that people who refuse to grow, however troublesome to us as pastors, are still people, loved and purchased by God at the cost of His Son. There is a treasure in that earthen vessel. They cannot be simply removed; they must be repositioned.

Repositioning a person who used to serve in a high level of leadership into another form of valuable ministry is the kindest and most responsible thing a senior pastor can do. Something in the life of that person originally qualified him for service—character as well as ministry ability and skill. Just because an elder can't "make the jump" doesn't mean he should be finished in ministry. Just the opposite is true. This person, handled properly, can be a valuable minister in the house and a powerful ally for the remaining elders.

The difference between legalism and grace is more than a simple theological proposition. In fact, while most people cannot articulate the theological underpinnings of either term, they most certainly can spot churches or leaders in the church that tend toward legalism. They can make these confident assertions because they can easily read the signs. It all boils down to how we treat people.

Legalistic leaders use people and discard them when they no

longer see eye to eye. To them, the principle is always more important than the person. They might even view a former elder as a threat, especially if that elder had to step down because he chose not to shift to the next level. In these cases the subtle signal sent to all is "don't cross me or you could wind up like Frank!" Legalism creates an environment of death, and neither people nor churches grow in such an environment.

A "grace" leader sees the former elder through the eyes of faith. Not at all threatened by him, the "grace" pastor sees a person who has made invaluable contributions to the church. He sees a person on a journey, a journey that led the former elder through a period of service on the eldership team. He also sees a friend whose life journey is not over. When the pastor finds a new place for the former elder to serve, a subtle signal is also sent to the rest of the congregation, but this one says, "This is a safe place. We believe in you because we believe that God has a plan for you. You can take risks here. Failure is not fatal." Grace breeds life. People and churches thrive in that kind of environment! Choose grace. Reposition the elder.

There may come a time when elders can no longer serve in that capacity, simply because they have chosen to live in the past. While they have made themselves no longer useful to the eldership team, they are still useful to God. It is our job as leaders to help these people find a place in the church that will allow them to prosper and continue to serve as a joint that supplies "according to the proper working of each individual part" (Ephesians 4:16 NASB). I would suggest a series of open and honest conversations between the senior pastor and the elder in question, the point of which is to find the place where the elder can serve and grow—a place where that person can experience fulfillment and excitement in making a contribution to the body.

3. "HOW DO I IDENTIFY AND RAISE UP NEW LEADERS?"

Many great books have been written on this subject, but a few thoughts here are in order:

First, without a continual supply of healthy new leaders, a local church cannot sustain a pattern of growth. This is another version of the chicken and the egg syndrome. Elevating leaders to new levels of leadership creates "space" for others to come into ministry. Bringing new people in to fill the ranks in the vacated areas attracts more people into service. This type of organizational movement creates what I call an "upward" draft. This produces a growth environment.

A growth environment attracts new people because it makes the church more attractive. As people visit, they can feel the life in the church. As more people join, new leaders have to be raised up. So what comes first, the new leaders or the new people, who by their presence "force" us to train new leaders? It is hard to say, but one thing is for sure: Growing churches are those that constantly train new leaders.

Second, there are at least four points of consideration when attempting to bring new leaders forth in the local

> **Growing churches are those that constantly train new leaders.**

church. The most important factor is the church's "imprint" or "DNA stamp." The most successful companies are those that have created their own "culture." In these companies, the way of doing business is not so much governed by a policy manual as it is by the culture of the company. These organizations have built into the systems that run them a certain philosophy of business life— how to treat employees, how to handle customers, a particular view on service, an unspoken understanding of family/work balance, etc. Often, new employees undergo extensive training programs immediately after being hired for the express purpose of imprinting them with the culture of the company—the "GE culture," for example.

Local churches need to do the same—imprint new leaders with the same DNA stamp inculcated into the church through the philosophies of the senior pastor. Some churches, for example, project an open-collar, laid-back approach that speaks to Gen X. Other churches might take on the starched-shirt, "type-A" feel, which might attract successful baby boomers. In both of these examples, the ramifications of these snapshots are many in terms of how these churches "do church"—how they communicate, use technology, balance work and life, and choose architectural features and everything else affected by style, including music, use of drama, etc.

How does a senior pastor discern his own DNA and therefore the DNA of the church? He begins with values. What is most important to him? What is of lesser or little value? List these and prioritize them. Examine the history of the congregation and its social or demographic context. Write down some key points concerning these ideas. Also include a list of theological non-negotiables and their implications in regard to church life. The compilation of the three lists provides the material for a first draft on your DNA.

Corporations have no choice but to hold special training classes in an effort to imprint incoming employees, but there is a better way. The truth is, some things are better "caught than taught." Take your time with those in leadership training. Some engraft your values faster than others. As people demonstrate that they possess the DNA imprint of the house, fold them into leadership positions.

The second point of consideration is an old cliché, but still true. Look for people who are FAT—faithful, available, and teachable. Do not be deceived by talent, giftedness, and ability. Though they may be gifts from God, they speak nothing of a person's character. Character is king! I have been burned a number of times by elevating talented people into positions of leadership only to find out later that I promoted them above their character cap. Look for character; skills can be added later.

The third point seems obvious but is often neglected by pastors: accountability. Once we find the right people and put them in the right spot, the tendency is to put them on autopilot, turn them loose, and forget they are there. Remember, anything left alone will revert to form. Without accountability and further training, even the best leaders will tend to slip backward. I once heard it said that people don't do what you expect; they do what you *inspect*.

The final point is related to the third. Provide opportunities for leaders to have contact with you, the senior pastor, in an environment all their own, for the purpose of keeping the vision before them. Faithful workers easily lose the forest for the trees, but what gives true meaning to ministry is how that single operation connects to the whole for the furtherance of the kingdom on earth. In these settings, the senior leader has the opportunity to voice gratitude to the other leaders in the house, all the while readjusting their focus onto the big picture once again. Happy, excited leaders attract others into leadership. And the cycle repeats itself.

What If the Church Is Not Growing at All?

CHAPTER SEVEN

EVERYTHING I HAVE SAID so far relates to growing churches. The sad truth is, most churches have plateaued for one reason or another and are not growing. For many, it has nothing to do with hitting a growth barrier. They are dealing with non-growth-related problems. Something has gone wrong, and active membership has leveled off—or worse, is in decline. Fully exploring this topic could fill volumes and include the writings of many experts in the field of church growth. To start, though, if a congregation is not growing, it is wise for leaders to analyze their church in terms of three areas: the "front door," functions and operations, and the "back door."

A. THE FRONT DOOR (LEAD COUNT, ASSIMILATION, PHILOSOPHY OF MEMBERSHIP, SYSTEMS)

Lead Count

Before dismantling everything in your church and copying some megachurch model, you should examine how you are doing with your "front door." The first question I always ask is, "What is your lead count?" In other words, "How many visitors do you have each week?" (Forgive the secular terminology. I believe there is both a scientific and a spiritual aspect to growing a church. Combine the two and the church will grow. Neglect one and the church will suffer.) Without new people coming, how can any church grow? Most church leaders do not even know they have a lead count problem!

My understanding of lead count came from a friend who owned a very successful transmission shop. He made lots of money each year from transmissions, a business from which he was able to retire at a young age. I once asked him why he was so successful. He replied with his stock answer, "I hire the best mechanics and pay them the best money in town." I didn't buy it, so I pressed him. "Wait a minute, no one knows that! No one says, 'I'm going to your shop because you pay your mechanics more.'" He then shared his secret with me. "Lead count," he said. "I am selling transmission jobs and I know what kind of salesman I am. Plus or minus a small percentage, I will sell a certain number of jobs per potential customer. So the key to making more sales is getting more people to come through that door—lead count. Raise the lead count, sales will go up, and I will make more money. I have the best lead count in town. In the end it all comes down to numbers, not transmissions." I immediately saw a correlation to the local church.

Studies show that the average church should aspire to keep up to 10 percent of the first-time visitors who walk through the front door. I have never seen a local church that consistently held that number—never. It is something to which one might aspire. (We are also told that we should keep roughly 25 percent of the visitors who come two consecutive weeks and almost 60 percent of the visitors who come three weeks in a row! The key is to get our guests to return a second and third time in a row!)

I often ask church leaders how many first-time guests they have each week but can count on my hands the ones who tracked such numbers. Those who had a rough idea were unaware of the value of these numbers. How can we discern if we have a front-door problem if we have no real idea what our lead count is? Let me explain. The following is not an attempt to be critical. This account is typical. My point in sharing it is to illustrate a point.

I once worked with a church that had declined from five hundred active members to four hundred over a five-year-period. My job was to help the leadership team discover the problems and reverse the trend. When I asked how many first-time guests they had each week, a short discussion ensued. The consensus was five first-time guest units (families or singles) each week. I explained that in the very best scenario, they might keep 10 percent of those first-time guests, and I wrote the following on a chalkboard:

5 guest units × 10% × 52 weeks = 26 units/year
26 units × 2.5 persons/unit (USA average) = 65 new members

I asked the leaders if they were happy about the potential of adding sixty-five individuals to the church each year. They were less than enthusiastic, and for good reason. First, their stated goal was to reach four thousand active members, which at sixty-five new members per year, would take over fifty-five years! And that was the good news! Actually, from the sixty-five new members, we needed to *subtract* the church's attrition rate. The attrition rate is the number of people who leave the church each year through death, transfer, or becoming inactive. Given that the church had declined one hundred members in five years, when the number of visitors indicated the church should have gained about three hundred members, the attrition rate clearly was outpacing any growth. On top of that, we started with the assumption that this church kept 10 percent of all first-time visitors. The church had a front-door problem. Their lead count was far too low.

If your church only has a few guests per week, I would suggest focusing your research and efforts in areas pertaining to attracting newcomers; in other words, increasing the lead count. The list below is in no way complete. Its purpose is to provide fodder for discussion and a potential spark toward creativity so leaders in local churches can discover ideas and methods that best fit their church culture and demographic context. (Again, as stated in chapter 4, our purpose is not just to put more people in the seats. Our job is to populate heaven by bringing people into the saving knowledge of Jesus Christ, and then to disciple them to change their world. A large lead count means a larger pool of potential disciples!)

1. Advertise a great preaching series. Send out thousands of first-class postcards to homes all over the community, usually to designated zip codes, inviting people to a seminar on Sunday mornings. The subject and titles of the messages should be driven by some felt need of the community, something people would be drawn to hear. Advertise childcare and any other element of your service that guests might perceive as a benefit. Make sure that the series lasts at least four weeks, since the goal is to bring guests back for at least three weeks in a row.

2. Hold a "friend day." Put together a special program for a certain day and then ask members to bring their friends to the event. In most cases, potential invitees are identified long in advance of the event and members are asked to record the names on a prayer card. Members pray daily for those on the list not only to come to the event but to come to Christ as well. One church turned their friend day into fall festival, which over the years has been very successful in attracting new members.

3. Try servant evangelism. This idea centers on the notion that barriers to the gospel in the minds of the lost are, in part, the result of misunderstanding the gospel's true message. The church in our time is at least partly guilty for these distortions. We have inadvertently communicated that people have to "get their lives together" in order to go to heaven. The truth is just the opposite: To go to heaven, one must acknowledge his or her sinfulness and great need for God. Then the person turns in faith and repentance to the Savior, who came to save us from our plight. He came because He loves us, no strings attached. He came to save us, not to tell us to get our lives together. Servant evangelism seeks to communicate this message through simple acts of kindness done with no strings attached.

Our church has touched thousands this way and received untold numbers of responses and testimonies as a result, not to mention a greatly increased lead count. Members might wash cars for free (no donations accepted), rake leaves, clean bathrooms in businesses, give away cold drinks or candy bars; the list is endless. We have cooperated with the organizers of local parades, festivals, and school events to provide water and/or cold drinks at no cost to thousands—people the organizers spent lots of money to attract!

With our acts of kindness we hand out small folded cards

that say, "Why are we doing this?" on the front. When the recipient opens the card, the inside reads, "We just wanted to show you the love of God in a practical way, no strings attached!" On the back we have our church's name, phone number, and a small map. Originally we left that information off the card but found people were skeptical and not as receptive without it.

4. Use invitations. Different types of invitations are useful. One is a general invitation to visit the church. Pastors often encourage members to invite others to church but rarely provide tools to empower them. Have a nice folded invitation card printed and put the picture of the pastor and spouse somewhere on the front. Those who make their living in print media will readily attest that photos attract interest. On the inside should be a well-worded invitation from the pastor, along with all necessary contact information for the church. On the back it is good to include a simple gospel presentation so the invitation doubles as a tract. (Make sure that every component of the invitation looks professional. The church is making a statement concerning who you are and who you aren't with this little card! Make it five-star in quality.)

Another type of invitation might come in the form of a ticket to an event. We have found over the years that people value a ticket, even if the event is free. So we produce them for major events, including Easter and Christmas productions. The tickets actually look like regular tickets and contain all the information a guest might need—the title of the event, times, location, information on childcare, other contact information, etc. Two Sundays before an event, we place the tickets in packs of five on the platform steps in the worship center. After announcing how we plan to present the gospel during this event, people can come up front to take as many tickets as they can distribute. When all of those people stream forward, the momentum is powerful, and the enthusiasm for outreach is contagious.

Thousands of people are invited through this low-cost method, but the biggest benefit is in mobilizing the membership to participate in the work of outreach. When church members invite their friends, neighbors, co-workers, etc., it shows the community that "something exciting must be going on over there if the people are so enthusiastic." Even if folks cannot make the event, the effect is not lost. The more a person is invited by various members, the greater the magnetic draw toward the church.

5. Host community events. While community events such as scout meetings, community watch gatherings, and AA meetings are not truly church events, they can be helpful tools for making your front door more open. People have a natural fear of going someplace new—especially a church. They aren't sure where the childcare is located or how children are checked in. They don't know where the bathrooms are (which is no small point!). They don't know what the place is like inside and might fear feeling trapped, because leaving shortly after arriving would be embarrassing to them. If, however, people come to a community event held on your church property, all these fears are assuaged. Make sure your property is in top shape when playing host. Make sure there is enough exciting information about your church for folks to feel drawn back for a Sunday service.

6. Advertise. Some people are turned off by the idea of a church advertising itself, but the truth is, we are already advertising ourselves. In some form or another, we make impressions on the community. The question is, what kind of message are we sending? And are we doing it by accident or intentionally?

When we plant a new church, we always create a first-class brochure and mail it to as many addresses as we can in the community. We want to define ourselves before the rumor mill has a chance to define us. Sure it is costly, but refurbishing a tarnished or distorted reputation is even more costly in lost potential converts and members.

Develop an advertising strategy. Consider television, radio, direct mail, newspaper, billboards, bus placards, community real estate maps, Yellow Pages, etc. Experiment, and go with what works. In every case, make sure the material is professional. You don't want your ad to produce a negative result.

7. Have a Web site. More and more people today are doing their homework before they physically visit a local church. We have a good number of members who visited our Web site before they came through the front door. In fact, the Web site was a major factor in their decision-making process. Not to be redundant, but make sure the site is professional looking. Web-savvy people have little tolerance for technological mediocrity. Also make sure that the information on the site is up to date and that your vision is clearly portrayed. Do everything possible to accurately communicate who you are.

Assimilation

After examining the flow of newcomers and ways to increase that flow, the next front-door question I ask leadership teams is, "What is your assimilation process like?" This is a big topic! (We once devoted a half-day seminar to this topic alone for our network of churches!) If people are coming, what are you doing to encourage them to stay? How do they connect with the church? Do you have a process, a system, in place to follow up on those who visit? Are they greeted in the parking lot, at the door? How do you address newcomers in the service? Do you embarrass them (perhaps unintentionally)? How do you find out who is there? Is there a guest card? How do you get the card to them? How do you retrieve the card? What do you do with visitor information?

Assimilation is simply the process by which those who visit are folded in as active, participating members of the local church. In my view, this is more than making a "pew sitter" out of a person; an active, participating member is, in some way, involved in the ministry life of the church.

I see eight elements involved in assimilation:

1. The Parking Lot. Over the years I have read a number of statistics concerning how quickly people make decisions about their potential return to a local church. While the numbers vary—some say the decision is made within seven minutes of arriving on the property, others say fifteen minutes—the net effect is the same; a powerful, lasting first impression is made long before the guest hears the pastor preach. Having a parking lot ministry gives a powerful first impression advantage to a church. Consider the following guidelines for parking lot ministry:

- Appoint a well-organized, customer service-oriented person as the leader.
- Provide traffic safety coats, vests, or belts to help people who serve in this ministry stand out.
- Determine the flow of traffic and clearly mark the parking lot accordingly.
- Designate the best spots as guest parking for first-time visitors and parking for expectant mothers.
- Arm parking lot attendants with information about the church.
- Provide a shuttle for those parking at a distance in a large lot.
- Equip attendants with umbrellas for inclement weather.
- Park cars in a quick and orderly manner.
- Teach attendants to smile and greet everyone they see, even if the car windows are closed.

2. Five "Touches." A "touch" is a meaningful contact made by the church with the first-time guest. Over the years, experts have considered five to be the minimum number of touches, or meaningful contacts, needed to make a new person feel welcome. To be effective, these touches must be programmed into the routine operation of public services held by a local church. The following is a list of possible touches that could be incorporated into the public expression of a church:

- *Greeting in the parking lot.*
- *Greeting at the door.* This is a must! Don't use just any volunteer for this ministry. Choose individuals who really enjoy people and train them to heartily greet everyone who walks through the door. They should smile at, warmly greet, and shake the hand of *everyone,* guest and member alike. Obviously, this invaluable ministry will require leadership, coordination, and enough people to make sure all who enter are sufficiently greeted.
- *Greeting inside.* To make sure each person is greeted, some churches provide another touch by having ushers or another set of greeters distribute bulletins at the doors leading into the worship center.
- *Distribution of a guest packet.* I will provide details about guest packets in point 5, "Information Gathering," but let me say here that, done correctly, this can provide another touch. Along with helpful information about the church, a guest packet should include a guest card and perhaps even a coupon for a free gift, which would provide another touch.
- *Greeting time in the service.* A time during the service should be provided in which everyone is encouraged to greet those around them. Do not make special mention of guests during this time. I'll give specific suggestions on how to do that in

point 5 that follows. Fear of embarrassment is one of the leading reasons people give for not attending church. Simply tell the congregation, "Let's all stand up and shake someone's hand. Tell them your name and that you are glad to see them." When most of the folks have returned to their seats, move on to the next portion of the service.

- *Ministry during the service.* This is the most valuable yet most unpredictable, hardest-to-program touch. When God touches the heart of an individual, he or she registers an instant connection with the church. It would be nice to be able to guarantee that our music, our preaching, and our people would minister to everyone every week.

- *Children's ministry.* Make sure new people find out the basic procedures of your ministry to children—where to pick them up, what the approximate length of the service might be, how a parent is alerted in case of an emergency. Putting this and other information in a well-done brochure that is handed out by a friendly greeter or children's ministry worker goes a long way toward making a parent feel comfortable and, therefore, provides a valuable touch.

- *Free gift.* Some churches provide a free gift to every unit (family or single) who attends a service for the first time. Generally, a coupon to receive the gift is placed in the guest packet. The idea is to demonstrate, in a tangible way, the gratitude of the church toward the first-time guests. Since most churches do not provide such a gift, those that do communicate a "five-star customer service" attitude. Gifts may include a tape or CD of the sermon, a coffee mug embossed with the church logo, a book or booklet, a worship CD, etc. We provide a free mug or a free book and a free beverage from our coffee bar in the lobby.

- *"Bonus" touch.* If the pastor makes his way to where the gifts are dispensed after the service, he can personally greet each guest, providing one more valuable touch. Some say that personal contact with the senior pastor is the most powerful touch a local church can give to a first-time guest.

- *A phone call.* Using information gathered from the guest cards, a friendly member calls guests and thanks them for their visit and offers to answer any questions. Those who serve on the phone team should be trained in evangelism and provided with a packet that contains answers to common questions people might have about the church. It is best to attempt this phone call within 24 hours of the guest's first visit.

- *The pastor's letter.* Again, using information gleaned from the guest cards, a letter from the pastor is mailed to guests, thanking them for their visit and inviting them to attend again. Special mention could be made of upcoming events that might be of interest.

3. Signage. Most church members and many pastors don't think about the importance of signs on a church property because they don't need them personally. They already know when and where everything is. And many would question why signage is part of a discussion on assimilation. While adequate signage will not add members, *inadequate* signage serves as a deterrent to assimilation since it hinders new people from breaking into the circle of fellowship.

When people drive onto your property, are parking spots designated for guests? From the vantage point of these spaces, is it clear where people should go next? Can they easily find the worship center? The Sunday school rooms? The children's ministry area? Are the bathrooms clearly marked? Are service times posted? Can one easily find the church office? Are office times posted? If your campus includes several buildings, are those buildings clearly marked (e.g., "Youth Center," "Family Life Center," etc.)? Make it easy for people to connect, and make your property seem open and inviting by communicating through high-quality, attractive signs.

4. Children's Ministry. One time a man greeted me with a clipboard in one hand and the other hand stretched toward me. "Well," he said, "my family and I will be joining your church!" I told him I was grateful and welcomed him into the fold, but I could tell he was eager to explain their decision. Looking at his clipboard, he continued, "The worship was okay and the sermon adequate, but from my survey, you have the best children's ministry I have seen. So this will be our church." I was not exactly overwhelmed by "warm fuzzies," but my curiosity was piqued.

It seems this family is among a growing trend of young families who are looking for excellent Christian training for their children. Fed up with Christian baby-sitting masquerading as children's ministry, these people are looking for quality. Fortunately for today's leader, there are a number of excellent companies that provide creative curriculum for the local church.

Make no mistake about it, quality ministry to children is a huge factor in how parents choose a church today. There is no invitation as powerful as a child exclaiming at the end of a service, "Mommy, I want to come back here next week!"

5. Information Gathering. Information is power. That's why everyone asks for it! Businesses offer huge giveaways to people who fill out a registration form with required fields that often include phone numbers and e-mail addresses. Today, people are skeptical of such ploys. Identity theft, the proliferation of scams, and fear of governmental control have accelerated their sense of caution. But there is no assimilation without follow-up, and follow-up is impossible without information.

I took our entire pastoral staff to a seminar on assimilation that featured a guest speaker from a very large and growing church. The speaker introduced his remarks with the claim that his church retrieved information from 40 percent of their guests. Forty percent of the visitors who were given guest packets turned in a guest card, and he could teach us to achieve the same. That's where he lost us. We routinely receive guest cards from 90 percent of our visitors! Not only do nine out of ten guests provide contact information, but they do it happily! What follows is a step-by-step presentation of our information-gathering mechanism:

- The pastor welcomes the guests: "I want to welcome everyone here today and I want to especially greet our first-time guests. We have prepared a guest packet for you, and we'd like to put one in your hands. We don't want to embarrass you, so we'll just ask you to do one simple thing. You see the ushers coming to the front. If you are a first-time guest would you just raise your hand until one of our ushers can hand you a guest packet and then you can put your hand down. That's as hard as it gets."
- Ushers quickly distribute the packets with a warm smile.
- As they do, the pastor continues: "Let me tell you what I'd like you to do with this packet. It contains lots of helpful information about our church, which you can read at your leisure. But first, please open it, look in the left-hand side and take out the card that says 'Guest Card.' Fill it out completely right away. And let me tell you why. After four brief announcements, I am going to receive an offering, and all that we ask you to put in the offering plate is the guest card, all filled out—nothing financial, just the card."
- The pastor continues: "After you finish filling out the guest card, look back in the packet, also on the left side, and take

out the coupon. This entitles you to receive a free gift. Why a free gift? Because we not only want to tell you we are grateful to have you here today, we want to demonstrate our gratitude in a tangible way. This gift serves as a token of appreciation and an indication of our desire for you to return and join us." He tells the guests what the gift is and instructs them on where it can be obtained at the end of the service.

- Finally, he instructs the congregation, "Let's make them feel welcome!" And the audience gives them a hearty ovation. Then we receive the offering.

So why does this work so well? Several key elements are included in this presentation. First of all, the offer of a guest packet filled with helpful information and the promise that it can be had without embarrassment is an attractive offer to first-time guests. Most raise their hands. Second, one of the top reasons people avoid church is the fear that they will be pressured for money. This presentation makes it clear that the guest can avoid the "money thing" altogether by just turning in the card. One nice byproduct of this arrangement is that it precludes the thought that "this church is just after my money." Further, when the offer of a free gift is given on the heels of telling guests that we don't want their money today, the first-timer gets the idea that the church is here to give and not get. The guest is made to feel special—like a guest!

Using this format we get about a 90-percent return on guest cards. How do we know? Simple: We keep track of how many guest packets were passed out that morning and count the number of cards that were turned in.

6. Follow-Up. The information you gather is the lifeline of your follow-up system. Without it, there simply is no follow-up. Not everyone who visits your church is called of God to stay there, but some are. The purpose of follow-up is to connect with those people.

Many pastors have no real plan when it comes to making further contact with guests. They figure that the people who want to come back will and those who don't, won't. I think this is irresponsible. God brought these people through your doors and you have a responsibility to do your best to connect them to life-giving ministry. In a very real sense, new people are to us what customers are to businesses, with one major exception. To a business, a customer is a source of revenue. To us, a person has eternal value. They must be born again and discipled in the context of a local church. Follow-up on our part is not optional. We must have a plan. Each local church will devise a plan that fits the personality of the church, but every plan should include three components:

- *Communication.* We have already suggested that guests receive a phone call and a letter from the church. Some churches make it a point to physically visit every person who visits them. Programs like Evangelism Explosion are excellent tools for training people for this type of ministry.

- *Evangelism.* Do not be afraid to be clear about what you believe and do not shy away from presenting the gospel to guests. This is a vital part of follow-up and assimilation. It not only provides the opportunity for unbelievers to come to faith in Christ, it also communicates to guests who are already believers and new to the area that you have an evangelistic priority. Believers who share this value are the kind of members you are looking for!

Develop an evangelism strategy and tie it in some way to the follow-up of your guests. Train leaders and recruit team members who enthusiastically serve in this vital aspect of the church's outreach and assimilation ministry.

- *Connections.* Getting people to connect with others in the church is the key to assimilation. The point is that newcomers must develop a relationship with someone in the congregation in order for them to connect in a long-term way with the church. Exciting music or great preaching may get them to come back, but they will only stick if bonded by the glue of relationship.

7. Connection Points. Some relationships "just happen," but this is rare. People have to be in proximity to others for a period of time for most people to connect. Local church leaders must be proactive in creating opportunities for people to "rub shoulders" with other people.

- *Food and fellowship go together.* Some churches have a meal on campus every week, while others may hold a newcomers' luncheon after church. The format should fit the culture of the church, but do not underestimate the power of food to cause fellowship to happen. Build into your calendar and annual budget connection opportunities that include food.
- *Pastor's class.* In *Surprising Insights From the Unchurched* (Zondervan), Thom Rainier outlines the indisputable role the senior pastor plays in the assimilation of new members into the church, especially formerly unchurched new members. One of the best ways to connect people to a church is through a "pastor's class." This mechanism allows new people to examine the belief system and vision of the church, connect with the senior pastor, and develop relationships with the other members of the class at the same time.
- *Small groups and Sunday school.* In my opinion, for true discipleship to occur on a wholesale basis in the church, some

form of small group is required. Ministry flows through relationships, and for ministry to be the ongoing, daily experience of a local church, life-giving relationships must be facilitated. A small group setting is ideal for this, whether it is a Sunday school class, Bible study, cell group, or weight-loss class. When true relationships develop, ministry can flow. As people's hearts become open to others, so do their lives. The give and take of life and ministry is what holds a church together. Paul says it best in Ephesians 4:16 (NIV): "From [Christ] the whole body, joined and held together by every supporting ligament, grows and builds itself up in love, as each part does its work."

8. Leadership Training. Assimilation is a full-cycle process that includes training the formerly unreached to reach and teach others. A growing church is constantly training leaders. Every ministry in the church must contain some mechanism where the next groups of leaders are being trained. Careful thought should first be given to assessing an individual's spiritual gifts to ensure a life-giving fit in ministry. Second, make opportunities for leadership and ministry available to those who have been trained. It is exasperating to prepare, complete the required training, receive a certificate, and then sit in the audience with nothing to do.

Philosophy of Membership

Do you have formal membership? How do people become members? Is this information readily available to newcomers? How many hoops do new people have to jump through to join your church? Are staff members and volunteers trained to help the assimilation process and answer any questions guests may have?

I encourage leadership teams to determine their philosophy of membership—what is needed for new people to connect with the church—and develop a *system* to facilitate this. Simply putting some really great people on the task requires constant maintenance and oversight, since the process is people-driven. One pastor told me, "Oh, we have a great assimilation process. We have a lady who takes all the cards and contacts visitors herself every Sunday afternoon." I replied, "What if she is sick or on vacation?" He had a procedure that was very dependent on one person to make it happen. He had no system.

Systems

A system runs all by itself. Wal-Mart has a system for receiving returned merchandise. It is the same in every store. Wal-Mart is known for being a well-run company, not because they hire really sweet people, but because they have a system. When you fly from city to city, the airline knows which seat you occupy not because a really smart counter agent remembered you, but because they have a system.

Create a system to facilitate the assimilation of new members into the church. As you incorporate aspects of what has been listed above, make sure each addition is not just "super-added" to the whole. Take the time to build each component into an overall assimilation system. This will save time and energy later as the church continues to grow.

Frustrated at one point, I took a pastor friend to lunch who was known for keeping a large percentage of people who visited his church. I furiously took notes as he outlined his whole process. Then I returned to the office and modified much of what he said to fit our church context. I created a system. Now we simply train folks to work the system (with plenty of customer service built in)!

B. FUNCTIONS AND OPERATIONS

I'm sorry, but some churches are just weird. They don't grow because they scare people away. Joseph Aldrich said that the main barrier to evangelism is not theological but cultural. I agree. Every church has its own tradition, even if its tradition is "non-tradition." There is nothing wrong with tradition, even if it is based on a departure from the lifeless religion of our past. The unfortunate thing is that often we ascribe theological meaning to what began as a pragmatic structure employed to facilitate life. The result is a "sacred cow," a religious structure without which we cannot conceive of "doing church."

When the church was meeting in the pastor's living room, it was appropriate to go around the circle and ask members to introduce the friends they had brought. But now, with three hundred people, this procedure is embarrassing to the unsuspecting people who come and the poor folks who brought them. When everyone knew everyone, and ol' Bob would sometimes head down the middle aisle during worship just because he had a "quickening," all would knowingly smile at the harmless old brother who had his spiritual upbringing in a small Pentecostal farm revival. But now folks are afraid to bring family and friends, because they don't want to be cast in that light. I am not against the move of the Spirit, but as one friend puts it, "If it is God for one, it is God for all." When only the same select few are the ones who feel the move, I wonder if it is really a move or simply a religious exercise. David Morris, author and well-known worship leader used to say, "Worship is free for all, but worship is not a free-for-all."

Learn to ask "why" about the things you do in your services and in the daily operation of the church. What do you do best? Make sure you put your best foot forward. Center on your strengths; put them up front. Is worship weak? Feature teaching. Are your children's ministries strong? Play that card more often. Mobilize in the areas you are strong and build in the areas you are weak. If, in asking "why," you uncover a "sacred cow" or two, kill it and invite the neighborhood to a huge feast. It will increase your lead count and help the church grow.

Churches differ in their philosophical approach to ministry. Some are seeker-friendly. Others might follow a traditional "stained-glass" format driven by quiet reverence for God. Some churches embrace a worship style complete with a contemporary band and very modern sound. From classical to charismatic and Presbyterian to Pentecostal, make sure that your philosophy of ministry and worship style will take you where you want to go. Ask the tough questions. Why do we do what we do the way we do it? Are people offended by our "freedom," or are they stifled by our apparent lack of it? Remember, you don't have to offend people to make God comfortable and you don't have to offend God to make people comfortable.

C. THE BACK DOOR

Some churches lose folks as fast as they gain them. New members are added while old members walk out the back door. Shutting this "back door" is not so hard. The key to keeping members in the church is not great worship or great preaching. These, and other aspects of ministry, might be what attract people to your church, but they are not the reasons they stay. Thank God! It is overwhelming to think that every Sunday we must re-compete to keep members in the church by hitting a "home run" sermon or producing a new set of goose bumps with every song. People stay in a church because they have relationships with the people in the church!

If your back door is open, your structures designed to facilitate the development and maintenance of relationships are failing. Some churches have no intentional structure designed to promote relationships. When a church is very small, no intentional structure is needed, but as it grows leaders must pay attention to this vital aspect of church life. The church is not primarily an institution or a religious organization, and it is definitely not a building. The church is people. While folks might be attracted to a church because of what it offers, they stay because of the friendships they develop there.

As I mentioned earlier, our church is a cell church. Every Sunday we meet for public worship, but other than that, everything we do is done in the cell context. (In fact, even on Sunday mornings, our children's ministries are built on a cell framework.) One of the prime reasons we chose this format as a blueprint for building our church is the fact that cell groups are highly relational. The life of the cell is the flow of ministry in that cell, and true ministry flows along relational lines. Without strong relationships, cell groups will fail. So if cells are working, relationships must be strong.

A church does not have to be a cell church to build strong relationships, but it must be intentional in creating an environment that is conducive to fellowship and friendship-building. Many churches have used Sunday school very successfully in accomplishing this goal. In those churches, however, a Sunday school class is more than a class; it is a fellowship group, an incubator for relationships where people connect to more than the content of the lesson.

No matter the model—whether based on cells, departments, or Sunday school—all meetings and events must have relational time built into them. Those minutes at the beginning of a board meeting when it seems impossible to get the folks to stop fellowshiping are far from wasted. In fact, depending on the agenda, they may be the most important part of the meeting! Picnics, parties, cookouts, and retreats are great times for people to connect.

Ministry events can also be relational in nature. Our church is very aggressive in evangelism. In addition to regular ongoing evangelism, every year we hold a number of large events. We put people into teams, allowing for plenty of interaction among team members. Side by side they labor in the same vineyard, passing out cold soft drinks at a city event, washing cars, or perhaps distributing tracts. They battle the same difficulties and experience the victories—together. *Together* is the key. Then all the teams gather back at the church building and share reports. The whole thing has a family feel. We are building memories together. It would be so much easier to see the task of evangelism as a monolithic function—reach the lost. But if it, or any other ministry function, is framed carefully, it accomplishes two goals: (1) it performs ministry, and (2) it builds relationships.

Examine ministry structures, asking key questions: Is this ministry built in such a way as to promote the building of friendships among participants? Are people only involved in this ministry because they are committed to it, or do some come because they enjoy the fellowship as well as the ministry? Do these people get together for fellowship outside the confines of ministry? Remember, people stay in a church because they are committed to each other, not to the mission or vision of the church. Do not kid yourself; plenty of other churches in town have great vision and wonderful ministries, but they don't have the relationships that your members have developed over the years. Those relationships are with the friends who attend your church!

A great test to see how you are doing in this area is found before and after every service and every meeting in your church. Do people come late and leave as soon as it's over, or do they stick around and hang out? Are they difficult to gather for a meeting, or do they sit silently waiting for it to start? Is the roar of fellowship so loud that someone has to whistle or yell to get people's attention? I often commend the people for being hard to gather. I want them to love fellowship; they need it and others are attracted to it. A guest spoke at one of our conferences and intuitively diagnosed the health of our network based solely on the fact that the crowd came early to hang out and would never leave when the meetings finished! The stronger the relationships in a local church, the greater the retention rate. Understanding this dynamic is no doubt one of the reasons that guest pastor leads such a large church with such a small back door!

Church Life Is
a Team Sport

A FINAL WORD

SENIOR PASTORS multiply themselves through proper alignment with their leadership teams. The leadership team rises to a level of usefulness in the body—which they would never have attained otherwise—when they function in right relationship to the senior pastor. When this happens, the body can better operate in its calling and produce growth on its own. The leadership of a church, like the bone structure of a natural body, needs to be healthy and properly aligned in order for the body to work as it should. Teamwork in the leadership promotes teamwork in the body, and that is what church life is all about—the body, building itself up in love (Ephesians 4:16). As elders release their senior pastor to lead, and as the senior pastor allows the leaders to help, the church will be positioned to pass through each barrier it faces, and they all can enjoy the ministry as they do it!

There are two reasons for growing a local church. The first is to produce a vehicle through which the kingdom of God may advance on the earth. If growth of a local church becomes a goal in itself, leadership has fallen into idolatry. Jesus established the church to further His cause in Jerusalem (the local area), Judea/Samaria (the region), and the uttermost parts of the earth. We seek growth for our churches so we can fulfill this mission more effectively—period. No other motive is acceptable. We are not after bigger churches so the pastor can build a name or so members can increase their impression of prestige in the community.

In addition, when the leadership of a church makes growth its number one aim, they miss the real secret of that growth and actually undercut the process. If they focus, however, on growing people and releasing them into ministry (the second reason for growing a church), the natural result is a numerical increase in active members. To make room for people to come into their destiny through service, the internal structures of the church will have to change. When these structures are readjusted and the leaders are properly aligned, more room is created for others. Growth results. Growth brings with it a need for change. Again, internal structures are readjusted and leaders realigned, creating more room for others. Again, growth results. It is a wonderful cycle leading to expansion on increasing scales.

God intended it to be this way. He never envisioned a small company of superstars extending His kingdom on the earth. From the start, He saw a body—His body—with many members, each doing its part to change the world.

Christianity is a team sport. We only have one superstar slot on the roster, and that position is filled! The rest of us serve as role players—each in his or her position, each doing his or her part—but we all share in the prize!

Michael Jordan was arguably the best player in NBA history. In his early days with the Chicago Bulls, Michael was a scoring machine and a one-man show. Coach Phil Jackson asked Michael to do an amazing thing. It seems that the team's winning percentage was far better when Michael scored fewer than thirty points per game. How could that be? When Michael scored in the thirty-point range, it meant other players had to step up and carry more of the load, so the men played more like a team. The result? Michael led the Bulls to six NBA titles.

When all of us play our position and do our part in the church, our Superstar, Jesus Christ, easily guides us to victory. And as we increase the number of players on the team, we increase the size of the team. In bolstering our numbers, not as spectators but as players, we bolster our resources in our quest to extend the kingdom of God on earth. Release people into their calling, and restructure your church to continue growing, all for the glory of God!